T0129195

Troubleshooting Xcode

Magno Urbano

Apress®

Troubleshooting Xcode

ISBN-13 (pbk): 978-1-4842-1561-6

ISBN-13 (electronic): 978-1-4842-1560-9

Managing Director: Welmoed Spahr
Lead Editor: Michelle Lowman
Technical Reviewer: Charles Cruz
Editorial Board: Steve Anglin, Louise Corrigan, James T. DeWolf, Jonathan Gennick,
    Robert Hutchinson, Michelle Lowman, James Markham, Susan McDermott,
    Matthew Moodie, Jeffrey Pepper, Douglas Pundick, Ben Renow-Clarke,
    Gwenan Spearing, Steve Weiss
Coordinating Editor: Kevin Walter
Compositor: SPi Global
Indexer: SPi Global
Artist: SPi Global
Cover Photo: Martijn Vroom

Distributed to the book trade worldwide by Springer Science+Business Media New York, 233 Spring Street, 6th Floor, New York, NY 10013. Phone 1-800-SPRINGER, fax (201) 348-4505, e-mail orders-ny@springer-sbm.com, or visit www.springeronline.com. Apress Media, LLC is a California LLC and the sole member (owner) is Springer Science + Business Media Finance Inc (SSBM Finance Inc). SSBM Finance Inc is a Delaware corporation.

For information on translations, please e-mail rights@apress.com, or visit www.apress.com.

Apress and friends of ED books may be purchased in bulk for academic, corporate, or promotional use. eBook versions and licenses are also available for most titles. For more information, reference our Special Bulk Sales–eBook Licensing web page at www.apress.com/bulk-sales.

Any source code or other supplementary materials referenced by the author in this text is available to readers at www.apress.com/9781484215616. For detailed information about how to locate your book's source code, go to www.apress.com/source-code/. Readers can also access source code at SpringerLink in the Supplementary Material section for each chapter.

Contents at a Glance

Contents

About the Author

Magno Urbano, with more than 20 years of experience in his field, is a longtime digital artist who has received many awards.

Magno Urbano started his professional life by graduating as an Electrical Engineer from USU (Brazil) but decided to switch gears and follow other fields that seemed more interesting at the time, like software engineering and, later, computer graphics and visual effects.

He has worked for almost a decade in the Visual Effects & Post Production Department of Globo Network TV (GNT) and later in the Multimedia Department of RTP (Radio and Television of Portugal).

Prior to this volume, Magno has written 15 books on multimedia themes and authored nearly 100 articles and 50 multimedia courses for the most important magazines in Europe and South America.

He has been working as an official beta-tester for Adobe since 2005.

Magno has been developing iOS and Mac OS X applications since 2008. During this period, he has developed and published about 100 applications for these platforms, some of them hitting #1 or placing in the top 10 in multiple countries for several weeks. His apps can be seen at http://addfone.com/magnourbano.

Right now, he is firing on all cylinders, excited to deliver his first book published by Apress!

Magno can be reached at troubleshooting-xcode@addfone.com.

About the Technical Reviewer

Charles Cruz is a mobile application developer for the iOS, Windows Phone, and Android platforms. He graduated from Stanford University with B.S. and M.S. degrees in engineering. He lives in Southern California and runs a photography business with his wife (www.bellalentestudios.com). When not doing technical things, he plays lead guitar in an original metal band (www.taintedsociety.com). Charles can be reached at codingandpicking@gmail.com and @CodingNPicking on Twitter.

Preface

Troubleshooting Xcode is a guide for those who are creating applications for iOS or OS X. The book contains solutions for hard problems—problems that any developer using Xcode will face, sooner or later.

Xcode is the official tool created by Apple for developing iOS and OSX applications. However, the limitations of this tool, several bugs, its enigmatic error messages make using Xcode, sometimes, very difficult.

To make things worse, some key documentation is incomplete, vague, or difficult to decipher.

To make life easier, first for himself, the author decided to make notes on all these problems and their respective solutions. Week by week, month by month, years of notes grew and Troubleshooting Xcode was born.

Troubleshooting Xcode also shows you how to automate some repetitive tasks and how to solve problems outside Xcode that are related to iOS or OS X development.

The code in this book is compatible with iOS 9 and OS X 10.11 "El Capitan." For that reason, the Swift code shown in this book is compatible with Swift 2.0.

We hope this book helps you to solve some of the hard questions you had during development. Some of these problems have multiple solutions and we have tried to add all options we know for each case. For that reason, this book is not a final guide for every solution. We are just doing our best.

Feel free to contact the author directly at `troubleshooting-xcode@addfone.com` if you want to suggest some topic to be added to future editions of this book.

Troubleshooting Xcode

Fighting Back

Because the development problems we describe are complex, this book is not a definitive guide to all problems with Xcode, iTunesConnect, and the Developer Portal.

The problems you will face during development are interconnected. Sometimes more than one issue can cause the same error message. We hope this book helps you solve most of these problems and gives you the insight to solve others we have not mentioned.

So, prepare your boxing gloves and let the first round begin.

Xcode Crashing when Opening a Project File?

This kind of crash is generally a sign that the project file is corrupted.

Unfortunately, due to Xcode's internal issues and bugs, projects get corrupted very easily, especially complex ones. A complex project using Auto Layout is an explosive combination that will lead to project corruption sooner or later. Probably sooner.

The most common cause for this problem is a corruption of internal files related to the project's workspace. These internal files can be easily removed to make the project fine again.

There are several steps available to solve the crashing problem.

If you are not using CocoaPods

1. Back up your project folder.

2. Locate the project file inside the project's folder (the one with a xcodeproj extension).

3. Right-click the project file and select **Show Package Contents**.

4. Delete project.xworkspace file and xcuserdata directory.

That's it. Try to open the project file now and Xcode will not crash.

> **Note**   **The bad news** is that Xcode uses these files and directories you have deleted to store workspace information (which windows and tabs are open and some debugger settings).
>
> **The good news** is that your code is intact and the files you have deleted will be re-created the next time you open the project.

If you are using CocoaPods

1. Execute steps 1 to 4.

2. Return to your project's folder and delete the file with a xcworkspace extension.

3. Also delete the Podfile.lock file on the same directory.

4. Launch Terminal in your project's folder, type the following command, and press the Return key:

```
pod deintegrate
```

Note Terminal is a program included with all versions of Mac OS X. It is located in the Utilities folder within the Applications folder. When launched, it provides a way to control the underpinnings of any UNIX-based operating system, like Mac OS X.

To launch the Terminal application, click Spotlight, type `terminal`, and press the Return key.

To switch Terminal to your project's folder, type the following command and press the Return key:

```
cd /thePathToYourProject
```

If the path contains spaces, you must precede every space with a backslash.

Example `/Mobile Documents` must be written as `/Mobile \ Documents`.

Note If you do not have `deintegrate` installed on your system, launch Terminal and type the following command:

```
sudo gem install cocoapods-deintegrate
```

5. Return to Terminal, type the following command, and press the Return key:

```
pod install
```

This will reinstall all pods your project is using and restore the `xcworkspace` file.

Now you can open the workspace file again and Xcode will not crash.

Note When you use CocoaPods your project file is the one with the `.xcworkspace` extension.

The Identity Used to Sign the Executable Is Invalid

Figure 1. Identity used to sign is invalid

This error message suggests that a signing identity is no longer valid or there is a problem with the device's clock. Even Xcode is not sure about the issue.

You can confirm the validity of all signing identities by visiting the Developer Portal, but I can bet there is nothing wrong with them.

We have seen this error before and the solution involves re-creating the provisioning profiles.

Follow these steps:

1. Launch Terminal, type the following command, and press the Return key:

   ```
   cd  ~/Library/MobileDevice/Provisioning\ Profiles
   ```

   This line will place Terminal inside the directory where Xcode stores the provisioning profiles.

2. Locate all provisioning profiles related to your project by typing the following command and pressing the Return key:

   ```
   grep -alir "XXXXX" *
   ```

   where XXXXX is the bundle ID of your application.

For example,

```
grep -alir "com.myCompany.myGreatApp" *
```

3. Delete all files found while executing the last step by typing the following command and pressing the Return key for every file found:

```
rm YYYYY
```

   where YYYYY is the filename to be deleted.

4. Using the Developer Portal, regenerate all provisioning profiles related to the project but give them new names.

5. Download the new certificates and drag them into Xcode's icon.

6. Restart Xcode.

Xcode Fails to Compile and Blames "SBPartialInfo"

The file myapp-SBPartialInfo.plist couldn't be opened because there is no such file

When you present an error message to the user, the general consensus is that

1. If the user can solve the problem, tell him how to do it.

2. If the problem is with a file created by the user, explain how the user can fix the file.

3. Never present error messages that talk about files the user has not created and about problems the user cannot solve. Why create confusion?

This error message violates all commonsense rules because it mentions a file that the user did not create; a file that the user has no knowledge of. Worse than that, the user cannot guess the problem even by consulting the most powerful Ouija board available.

After a few years using Xcode, we know that several problems can cause this kind of error message. The first problem is that there is something wrong with an Auto Layout constraint.

Problem with a NSLayoutConstraint

Most of the time, this SBPartialInfo error has to do with a problematic NSLayoutConstraint. Yes, you read correctly, the good and old Auto Layout constraint, our crash buddy.

To solve this problem, follow these steps:

1. Select the **Report Navigator**, by clicking the last icon of the top part of Xcode's Project Navigator panel (Figure 2) or by pressing ⌘8.

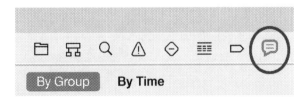

Figure 2. Report Navigator

2. Select the top report and read it carefully, until you find the offending NSAutoLayoutConstraint.

There is also another kind of problem that can cause the error message seen in Figure 1: an incorrect path to the Info.plist file.

Incorrect path to Info.plist

Check your target's **Build Settings** if the path to your Info.plist file is correct.

Select the target in question **(1)**, click **Build Settings (2)**, select the **Packaging** section **(3)**, and check whether the **Info.plist** file line **(4)** has the correct path and name of your Info.plist file (see Figure 3).

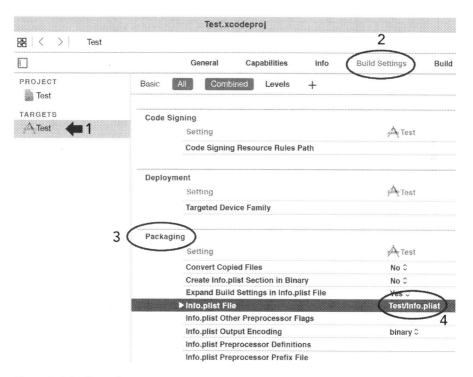

Figure 3. Info.plist path

There is a third kind of problem that can also cause the error message seen in Figure 1: having the Info.plist file assigned to a target.

Info.plist must NOT be assigned to a target

Select the Info.plist file on Xcode's Project Navigator (Figure 4) and on Xcode's right panel, click the File Inspector icon (marked with a circle in Figure 5). On the same right panel shown in Figure 5, make sure that you have not assigned the Info.plist file to any target (see arrow).

Figure 4. Info.plist location

Figure 5. Do not assign the Info.plist to any target

Note   Do **NOT** assign the Info.plist to any target.

Duplicate references to the storyboard file

If you have performed extensive changes to your project, like duplicating targets, renaming storyboards, renaming files, and so on, the Gods will not like you and they will become angry. Be assured that they will punish you by corrupting some file here and there or forgetting to update something essential on your project file.

One of these punishments happens when you rename a storyboard and Xcode "forgets" to remove the old storyboard reference from the Info.plist file. Now you have an Info.plist file with two storyboard references, one valid and one invalid. You can guess that things will start to get ugly very soon . . . .

Believe us; bad things will happen sooner than you think.

You may solve this problem by right-clicking the Info.plist file (Figure 4) on the Project Navigator panel and choosing **Open As ➤ Source Code** (Figure 6).

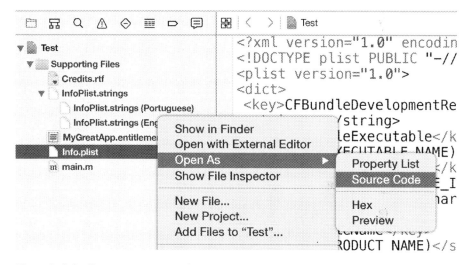

Figure 6. Info.plist seen as source code

Look for duplicate lines like the following in the source code:

```
<key>UIMainStoryboardFile</key>
<string>Main</string>
```

These two lines tell you that the storyboard filename (UIMainStoryboardFile) is "Main" (Main.storyboard).

Only one reference like this must exist inside Info.plist. Delete all other references and save the file.

No Matching Provisioning Profiles Found

The error message shown in Figure 7 appears when you try to submit an application to the App Store. The occurrence of this message relates, generally, to two things: an expired or a missing provisioning profile.

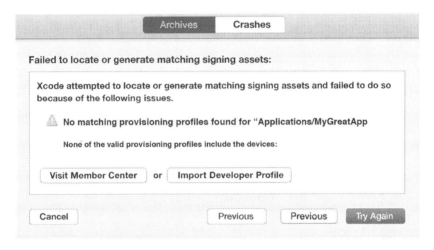

Figure 7. *Failed to locate signing assets*

Missing provisioning profile

From time to time, the Gods wake up on the wrong foot and decide to delete or revoke some of your provisioning profiles. "Everything was just working fine yesterday," you say. We know.

First, verify whether you have configured Xcode with the correct provisioning profiles for the selected target by navigating to the project's Build Settings tab (Figure 8).

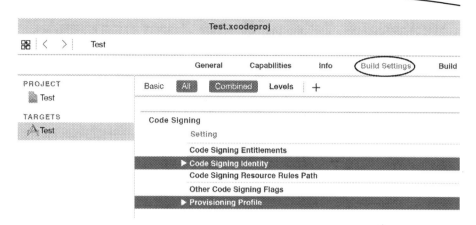

Figure 8. Code signing and provisioning profile

If the provisioning profiles are missing, download them from the
Developer Portal.

Note   OK, we could suggest that you let Xcode get the provisioning profiles for
you, automatically, but, unfortunately, this operation fails 99.99% of the time to
solve this problem. It is faster to download the provisioning profiles yourself.

Compressing Images Better Than Photoshop

If you love to compress your own images, here are some power tips.

As far as we know, the best application out there for image optimization and compression for Mac OS X is ImageOptim (www.imageoptim.com). ImageOptim is a free application that combines many optimization tools like PNGOUT, Zopfli, Pngcrush, AdvPNG, extended OptiPNG, JpegOptim, jpegrescan, jpegtran, and Gifsicle on an easy-to-use interface.

Xcode is configured, by default, to compress all images added to the bundle, but the results are not as good as those of ImageOptim.

In order to use your own compressed images, you have to disable Xcode's compression flag, by disabling **COMPRESS_PNG_FILES** on the **Build Settings** tab. Change this option from **YES** to **NO** to prevent Xcode from compressing the images you have already compressed (Figure 9).

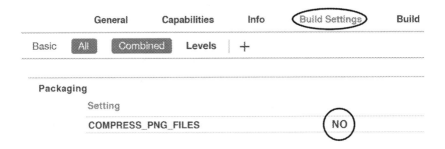

Figure 9. Compress PNG option

Creating Packages for in-App Purchases

You have decided to add in-app purchases to your application. The in-app purchases will deliver content to the user and Apple will host the content. How do you do that?

Delivering content

Before the release of iOS 6, developers were responsible for keeping and delivering content to users after purchase. All content was to be stored on servers maintained by the developers themselves.

Since Apple introduced iOS 6, it is possible to host all content with Apple, making the process easier.

To submit your content to Apple, you must pack all content in a special kind of file called "package."

What is a package?

In simple words, a package is a structured folder. Inside this folder is a file called ContentInfo.plist and a folder called Contents.

ContentInfo.plist

The ContentInfo.plist file contains two keys:

- **ContentVersion**, which represents the version number of the content;

- **IAPProductionIdentifier**, which is the in-app purchase bundle identifier, something like com.myCompany.myInAppPurchase.

Contents folder

The Contents folder contains all files related to a particular in-app purchase, like music, videos, images, texts, and so on, that are associated with the content you are selling.

> **Note** You can have any kind of content inside your in-app purchase, except code.

Creating a package, the faster way

Apple recommends using Xcode to create packages for your in-app purchases, but the process requires endless clicks and a maze of configurations.

We have created another way for you, easier and suitable for bulk delivery.

Here we go:

1. Using Mac OS X Finder, create a folder with the name of your in-app purchase's bundle identifier, something like `com.myCompany.myApp.pack100`. Let's call this folder the main package folder.

2. Create a folder called `Contents` inside the main package folder.

3. Create a plain text file named `ContentInfo.plist` inside the main package folder.

At this point, you will have a structure like the one seen in Figure 10:

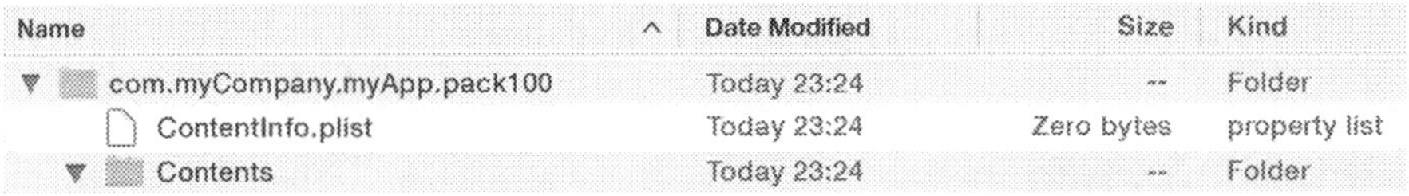

Name		Date Modified	Size	Kind
▼ 📁 com.myCompany.myApp.pack100	∧	Today 23:24	--	Folder
📄 ContentInfo.plist		Today 23:24	Zero bytes	property list
▼ 📁 Contents		Today 23:24	--	Folder

Figure 10. In-app purchase package structure

4. Copy all multimedia content that the package will deliver to the `Contents` folder.

5. Add a structure like the following one to your `ContentInfo.plist` file:

```
<?xml version="1.0" encoding="UTF-8"?>
<!DOCTYPE plist PUBLIC "-//Apple//DTD PLIST 1.0//EN" ↵
        "http://www.apple.com/DTDs/PropertyList-1.0.dtd">
<plist version="1.0">
<dict>
        <key>ContentVersion</key>
        <string>1.0</string>
        <key>IAPProductIdentifier</key>
        <string>XXXXX</string>
</dict>
</plist>
```

Replace XXXXX with the in-app purchase's bundle ID, which, in this example, is com.myCompany.myApp.pack100.

The folder structure is now just like the one seen in Figure 11:

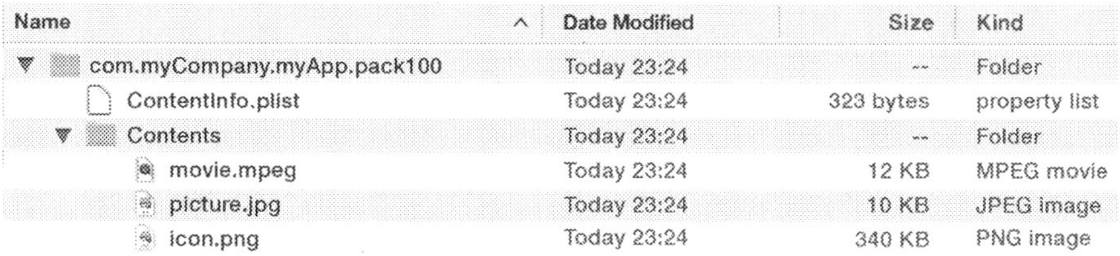

Name	^	Date Modified	Size	Kind
▼ 🔲 com.myCompany.myApp.pack100		Today 23:24	--	Folder
🗋 ContentInfo.plist		Today 23:24	323 bytes	property list
▼ 🔲 Contents		Today 23:24	--	Folder
🎞 movie.mpeg		Today 23:24	12 KB	MPEG movie
🖼 picture.jpg		Today 23:24	10 KB	JPEG image
🖼 icon.png		Today 23:24	340 KB	PNG image

Figure 11. In-app purchase final structure

Creating the final package

It is time to create the final package file with a pkg extension.

Launch Terminal in the folder that contains the main package folder, type the following command, and press the Return key:

```
productbuild --content <pathToInAppDirectory> ↵
            <pkg-name.pkg>
```

Example:

```
productbuild --content com.myCompany.myApp.pack100↵
            com.myCompany.myApp.pack100.pkg
```

This command will create the package for you in the same directory. You can submit this package later to Apple using Application Loader.

> **Note**   If the productbuild command fails it means that you have to install Xcode's command-line tools on your system. To do that, launch Terminal and type the following command:
>
> ```
> xcode-select --install
> ```

Reduce Up to 75% of the Compiling Time

One of the most time-consuming things about development is the time Xcode takes to compile, build, and run your application.

Depending on how you configure, it may be taking too long to compile your code.

One of these "wrong" configurations will force Xcode to generate files that are not necessary for development. One of these files is a dSYM file that contains debug symbols of your compiled code. Generating these files every time makes the compilation take a long time, unnecessarily.

You can disable the dSYM generation for development by selecting **Build Settings ➤ Build Options ➤ Debug Information Format ➤ Debug** (Figure 12) and changing this item from DWARF with dSYM File to DWARF (Figure 12).

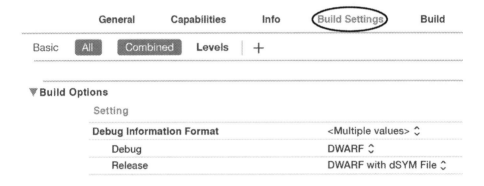

Figure 12. Debug information format

Note New projects created by Xcode 7 have this option configured as DWARF, meaning that Xcode will not create dSYM files during development.

Previous versions of Xcode have this same option set as DWARF with dSYM file, meaning that dSYM files will be created during development and the project will take longer to compile.

Note   If your project uses CocoaPods or deals with multiple target dependencies, don't forget to change this option for all targets.

You should keep DWARF with dSYM File for the **Release** option or you will not be able to symbolicate the crash logs when you get them from the App Store.

Note   During the process of symbolication of a crash log, Xcode combines the raw crash log file with the dSYM file and creates a human-readable version of the crash log. That friendly version of the crash log contains information about the code that the programmer can recognize and helps identify what caused the crash.

Impossible "Constants" in Objective-C

Unlike Swift, you cannot declare a collection like an NSArray, NSDictionary, and so on, as a constant using Objective-C; but we think we may have a solution for that.

The solution involves creating an NSObject-based class and declaring static variables to back up and simulate a "constant" collection.

Constants.h

```
#import <Foundation/Foundation.h>

@interface Constants : NSObject

+ (NSArray *) myConstantArray;
@end
```

Constants.m

```
#import "Constants.h"

@implementation Constants

+ (NSArray *) myConstantArray {
    // by declaring the static on the implementation we guarantee
    // that other classes using this one will not make their own copy of
        the static

  static NSArray *_myConstantArray = nil;
  @synchronized (_myConstantArray) {
    if (_myConstantArray == nil) {
      _myConstantArray = @[ /* declare your array here */ ];
    }
    return _myConstantArray;
  }
}
@end
```

To use this "constant," you must use the following form:

```
NSArray *anArray = [MyConstantClass myConstantArray];
```

Concurrency with Core Data

Sometimes your application may crash during Core Data operations without a clear reason.

One of the possibilities we will explore now is that the application may be accessing the NSManagedObjectContext object from different threads, simultaneously.

To access Core Data entities from multiple threads Apple recommends that you use thread confinement.

The pattern recommended for concurrent programming with Core Data is thread confinement: each thread must have its own entirely private managed object context.

There are two possible ways to adopt the pattern:

1. *Create a separate managed object context for each thread and share a single persistent store coordinator. This is the typically recommended approach.*

2. *Create a separate managed object context and persistent store coordinator for each thread. This approach provides greater concurrency at the expense of greater complexity (particularly if you need to communicate changes between different contexts) and increased memory usage.*

Before you spend time developing the necessary code to support thread confinement, you may want to confirm whether the problem your app is experiencing is really being caused by multiple threads accessing the Core Data context object at the same time.

The code

Basically, the code is a lock mechanism in place to control the context access. Just one thread will be able to access the context at the same time.

You must find the point in your code where you are accessing the context and add the following lines that are in **bold**:

Swift

Entity.swift

```swift
import Foundation
import CoreData

@objc(Entity)
class Entity: NSManagedObject {

    static let lock = NSLock()

  func allObjectsInContext(context : NSManagedObjectContext) ↵
              -> NSArray {
    var all : NSArray?

    // prepare a fetch request
    let request : NSFetchRequest? = NSFetchRequest()
    request?.entity = ↵
            NSEntityDescription.entityForName("Entity", ↵
                inManagedObjectContext: context)
    request?.returnsDistinctResults = true
        Entity.lock.lock()
      do {
        // this is where you are accessing the context
        all = try context.executeFetchRequest(request!)
        // success ...
      } catch let error as NSError { // failure
        print("Fetch failed: \(error.localizedDescription)")
      }
        Entity.lock.unlock()
    return all!
  }
}
```

Objective-C

Entity.h

```objc
#import <Foundation/Foundation.h>
#import <CoreData/CoreData.h>

NS_ASSUME_NONNULL_BEGIN

@interface Entity : NSManagedObject

+ (NSArray *)allObjectsInContext:(NSManagedObjectContext *) ↵
                                  context;

@end

NS_ASSUME_NONNULL_END
```

Entity.m

```
#import "Entity.h"

@implementation Entity

+ (NSArray *)allObjectsInContext:(NSManagedObjectContext *) ↩
                                        context
{
  NSArray *all = nil;

  // prepare a fetch request
  NSFetchRequest *request = [[NSFetchRequest alloc] init];
  request.entity = [NSEntityDescription ↩
                    entityForName:NSStringFromClass([self class]) ↩
          inManagedObjectContext:context];

  [request setReturnsDistinctResults:YES];

  NSError *error = nil;

  // this instruction will lock the context, preventing
  // multiple accesses to it

  @synchronized(context) {
      // this is where you are accessing the context
      all = [context executeFetchRequest:request error:&error];
  }

  return all;
}

@end
```

> **Note**   Be aware that this mechanism may slow down your application, especially if you are dealing with a database-intensive application. Use it for debug purposes only.

If your code stops crashing after you add the @synchronized line, then the problem is confirmed and we recommend that you follow Apple's recommendations and create independent contexts for each thread.

Creating Icons from Terminal

What about creating all icons for your iPhone, iPad, and Mac applications at once, in seconds, without almost any effort?

Good, isn't it? We have prepared two scripts for you: one for creating icons for your iOS applications and another for creating icons for your Mac applications.

Creating Icons for iOS Applications

The following script creates icons for iOS applications:

```
mkdir -p ./icons_iphone
mkdir -p ./icons_ipad
for x in 29 40 60
do
   double=$(($x * 2))
   triple=$(($x * 3))
   sips --resampleWidth $double icon.png --out ↵
                        ./icons_iphone/icon-$x@2x.png
   sips --resampleWidth $triple icon.png --out ↵
                        ./icons_iphone/icon-$x@3x.png
done

for x in 29 40 76
do
   double=$(($x * 2))
   sips --resampleWidth $x icon.png --out ./icons_ipad/icon- ↵
                        $x.png
   sips --resampleWidth $double icon.png --out ↵
                   ./icons_ipad/icon-$x@2x.png
done
```

> **Note**   This script will create two folders: one containing the iPhone and the other containing the iPad icons.
>
> iOS icons will be created with the following sizes: 29, 40, and 60 points @2x and @3x for iPhone and 29, 40, and 76 points @1x and @2x for iPad. Applications compiled for iOS 7 and up use these formats.

Creating icons for OS X applications

Use the following script to create icons for your Mac applications:

```
mkdir -p ./icons_mac
for x in 512 256 128 32 16
do
    double=$(($x * 2))
    sips --resampleWidth $double icon.png -out ↵
                ./icons_mac/icon-$x@2x.png
    sips --resampleWidth $x icon.png --out ↵
                ./icons_mac/icon-$x.png
done
```

> **Note** Mac OS X icons will be created with the following sizes (compatible with Mac OS X 10.8 and up): 16, 32, 128, 256, and 512 points at @1x and @2x resolutions.

Using the scripts

1. Create a big version of your application's icon with at least 1024 x 1024 pixels and save this image as icon.png to the Desktop folder.

2. Launch Terminal in your Desktop folder.

3. Copy (⌘C) and paste (⌘V) one of the scripts listed in this section to the Terminal window and press the Return key.

The script will execute and pause. Press the Return key again to resume the script.

> **Note** Instead of copying and pasting the codes every time you want to use them, you can use the scripts we have provided in this book and at apress.com.

UINavigationBar Tint Not Working

If you are trying to change the tint color of a navigation bar using the
tintColor property and the color is not changing, it turns out that the
navigation bar has another tint property called barTintColor. Instead, you
should use the methods shown next.

Swift

```
let bar = self.navigationController?.navigationBar
bar?.barTintColor = UIColor.greenColor()
```

Objective-C

```
UINavigationBar *bar = self.navigationController.navigationBar;
bar.barTintColor = [UIColor greenColor];
```

Debugging an Insanely Hard Quartz Error

If your project uses Quartz extensively and the code is crashing without giving you any clues to the problem, you will love this section.

There is hope...

A possible solution for debugging a complex Quartz application is to add a CGPostError breakpoint to your project.

Select the **Breakpoint Navigator (1)**, click the + at the bottom left of the pane **(2)**, choose **Add Symbolic Breakpoint (3)**, and fill the **Symbol** field with CGPostError (Figure 13).

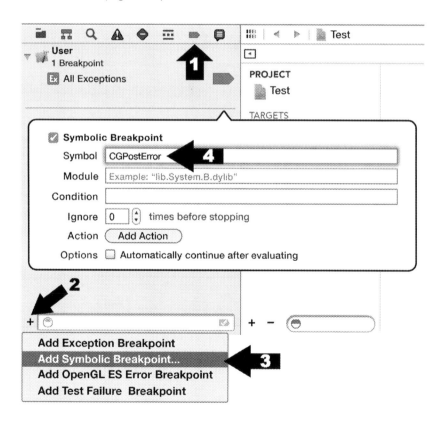

Figure 13. Add symbolic breakpoint

XCode will now stop at the offending lines if they are related to Quartz.

Adding Objects to an Array Concurrently

If you ever tried to add objects to an NSMutableArray concurrently you know that it is impossible. An NSMutableArray will not allow simultaneous access to its contents.

This Objective-C code, for example, will crash with the error message: "NSArray was mutated while being enumerated."

Objective-C

```
NSMutableArray *newArray = [[NSMutableArray alloc] init];

[anotherArray
    enumerateObjectsWithOptions:NSEnumerationConcurrent ↵
                    usingBlock:^(id obj, ↵
                                    NSUInteger idx, BOOL *stop)
{
  // add a new object to newArray
  [newArray addObject:newObject];
}];
```

The crash happens because the enumeration runs concurrently. Any two threads trying to add a new object to newArray at the same time will crash the application.

Old-School C

The solution is to use an old-school C array.

```
// cArray is an array of "id" elements
// count is the number of entries the cArray will have

id cArray [count];
id __strong *arrayPtr = cArray;

/* populate the array
   arrayPtr[0] = ...
   arrayPtr[1] = ...
   arrayPtr[2] = ...
   etc...
*/
```

```
[anotherArray ↵
    enumerateObjectsWithOptions:NSEnumerationConcurrent ↵
                    usingBlock:^(id obj, NSUInteger idx, ↵
                                    BOOL *stop) {
        arrayPtr[idx] = newObject;
}];
```

This solution works because as idx increments, a different memory
allocation of arrayPtr[idx] will be given for the enumeration. There is no
way for two threads to access the same memory address. For that reason,
this code will never crash.

Back to the future

You can later convert this C array into a regular NSMutableArray by using the
following:

```
NSMutableArray *array = [NSMutableArray ↵
                arrayWithObjects:cArray ↵
                            count:count];
```

> **Note**   Simultaneous access to an array in Swift works just fine and no
> additional code is necessary.

The App Is Damaged and Can't Be Opened

Following is part of the error message presented by Xcode: *Delete the app and download it again from the App Store.*

The Condition

We had a Cocoa application trying to validate its internal purchase receipt at launch, but we did not find the receipt inside the bundle.

Following Apple's instructions, we forced the application to quit using exit(173), which instructs iTunes to retrieve the missing receipt, but we still were not able to retrieve the receipt.

Following is what Apple has to say about receipt validation failure (http://addfone.com/TXReceiptValidation):

Respond to Receipt Validation Failure

Validation can fail for a variety of reasons. For example, when users copy your application from one Mac to another, the GUID no longer matches, causing receipt validation to fail.

Exit If Validation Fails in OS X

If validation fails in OS X, call exit with a status of 173. This exit status notifies the system that your application has determined that its receipt is invalid. At this point, the system attempts to obtain a valid receipt and may prompt for the user's iTunes credentials.

Several web pages on the Internet indicate how this problem relates to certificates, but we have experienced this problem several times before and have observed another condition that may also cause this error: **a corrupt sandbox user**.

The Gods want to punish you

You know the drill: one day you are happy, the sun is shining, the flowers are blooming, the birds are singing, and everything is working fine on Xcode.

The day after that, the Gods wake up on the wrong foot and punish you. Sometimes they punish you indirectly, by sentencing the sandbox user to a miserable death by internal corruption. When that happens, retrieving or validating purchase receipts for that user will fail.

As a bonus, the Gods will never present you with any error message that can provide a tip about the real reason for the problem—and you will never guess.

The solution for a dead sandbox user is to delete the offending user and create a new one via iTunesConnect.

Note Another possible solution you can try is to open the Mac App Store application (if you are dealing with a Mac application) or iTunes (if you are dealing with an iOS application), log out from the current account, and quit the application immediately after that.

Application Failing to Obtain a Receipt

You have created a new sandbox user as instructed in the previous section, but your application is still failing to obtain the purchase receipt?

Verify if your code is properly signed.

Go to the target's **Build Settings** and adjust the **Debug** and **Release** fields of **Code Signing Identity** and **Provisioning Profile** with the correspondent values for your application (Figure 14).

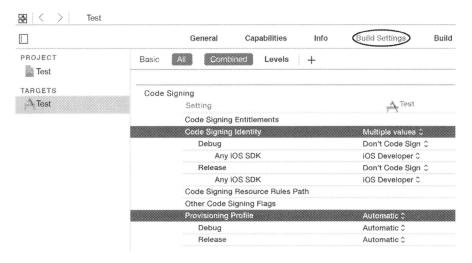

Figure 14. *Code Signing Identity and Provisioning Profile*

In Figure 14, you can see that the Provisioning Profile section is adjusted as Automatic for the **Debug** and **Release** entries. Click Automatic and change both entries to the respective target's provisioning profiles.

Also change the iOS Developer entries of the **Code Signing Identity** to the correct identities for **Debug** and **Release** that will appear after adjusting the **Provisioning Profile** section.

Classes with the Same Name on Different Targets

You have a project with multiple targets, specifically involving different platforms like iOS and OS X.

You have two classes called RenderMe, one designed for iOS and the other one designed for OS X. The classes are similar in functionality but the implementation is completely different, due to platform differences.

You want the classes to have the same name, because it simplifies project management and because they serve similar purposes.

At some point in development, you will have to assign the classes to their respective targets and import the classes using lines like the following:

```
#import "RenderMe.h"
```

This is what you expect...

You expect the iOS target to import and compile the iOS version of RenderMe, with the same being true for the Mac OS X target.

Not so fast!

Believe us, given the proper time and project complexity, Xcode will import and compile the wrong class for the wrong target. We have seen this before.

You have two solutions at this point: to have different names for the classes or to import them using absolute paths.

Instead of

```
#import " RenderMe.h"
```

for both targets, use lines like

```
#import "/absolutePathForMyIOSRenderMe/RenderMe.h"
#import "/absolutePathForMyMacRenderMe/RenderMe.h"
```

for each case. Ugly, but it works.

A Case Against Base Internationalization

iOS 6 introduced an option in Xcode called **Use Base Internationalization**. You can see this option by navigating to your project's Info tab (Figure 15). **Base Internationalization** works by defining a default language to be used as the base language.

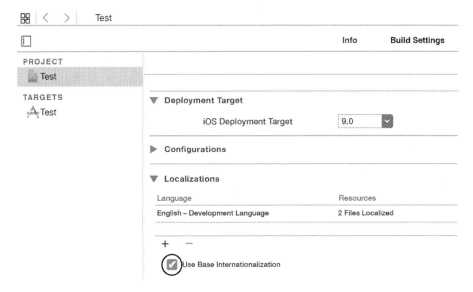

Figure 15. Use Base Internationalization

Suppose your application is localized in English and Portuguese and the former is the base language. All users that have their devices configured in Portuguese will see this localization, and all others will see the English one, because that is the base language.

Localization of interface elements

When we talk about localizing interface elements, we are talking about XIB files and storyboards.

Before iOS 6, localizing an interface file would make Xcode generate extra copies of the XIB and storyboard files, one per language being localized. That multiplicity of files made it almost impossible to maintain and work with multiple localizations.

Apple solved the problem by introducing an option called Base Internationalization. Using this option, instead of having multiple copies of interface elements, you now have one XIB or storyboard assigned as the base language and text files containing the localizations for the other languages (Figure 16).

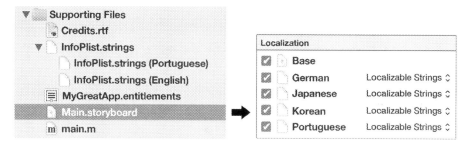

Figure 16. *A storyboard localized in multiple languages*

The idea of Base Internationalization is nice, but you must be aware that this feature has problems that prevent some interface elements from being localized.

Localization of UIBarButtonItem and other elements failing

One classic example of the Base Internationalization option failing to localize an element appears when your application uses UIBarButtonItem objects. The Base Internationalization option will not localize these elements automatically. Xcode will not even add their strings to the localization files, and adding them manually will not localize the elements.

If you use UIBarButtonItem objects you will have to localize them programmatically at runtime.

> **Note**   If you use the **Base Internationalization** option, be sure to test your application on all languages because some other interface elements, including UIBarButtonItems, may also not appear localized.

Checking for Missing Localizable.strings

You have localized an application for several languages, but you have the feeling that some strings are missing on one language or another.

Going through all localization files and comparing them is too complex and counterproductive.

We have good news: you can make Xcode check for missing strings for you!

Select **Product ➤ Scheme ➤ Edit Scheme** and add the option -NSShowNonLocalizedStrings YES to the **Arguments Passed on Launch** section (see Figure 17).

Figure 17. *Checking for missing Localizable.strings*

Next time you run the application, you will see the missing strings on Xcode's console, something like the following:

```
BarButtonItemColor[23980:60b] Localizable string "Ahi-1h-yfI.title"
not found in strings table "Main~iphone" of bundle CFBundle 0x17d70dd0
</var/mobile/Applications/1228CFF2-DB3D-4A2D-B0D8-17DA32E7DD8A/
BarButtonItemColor.app>
```

This error message is related to an application created initially in English (base language) and later localized to Portuguese.

The missing string on the error message belongs to element "Ahi-1h-yfI.title", which, **not by coincidence**, is a UIBarButtonItem, confirming what we have said in the section "A Case Against Base Internationalization."

After localizing the storyboard of that project from the base language to Portuguese, Xcode did forget to add the UIBarButtonItem's string to the localization files and this is why Xcode was complaining.

Adding the missing string to the Portuguese localization file will not localize the UIBarButtonItem. The only way to localize this button is to do it programmatically at runtime.

You Are Declaring Your NSString Wrong

You need to declare a constant NSString to use on your brand-new class and you are probably declaring it as shown next.

Objective-C

```
const NSString * kMyConstant;
```

This line gives you a **pointer to a constant** NSString. That is not what you are looking for, simply because NSString objects are already immutable.

Instead, you should declare it as follows:

```
NSString * const kMyConstant;
```

This gives you a **constant pointer to an** NSString, which is what you are looking for.

This is how you should declare your NSString constants.

> **Note**   To declare a constant in Swift all you have to do is declare it using the `let` keyword:
>
> ```
> let kMyConstant = "something"
> ```

CocoaPods: /Manifest.lock: No Such File or Directory

diff: /../Podfile.lock: No such file or directory

diff: /Manifest.lock: No such file or directory

*error: The sandbox is not in sync with the Podfile.lock.
Run 'pod install' or update your CocoaPods installation*

If your project uses CocoaPods and it is failing to compile with this error message, try the following:

1. Close Xcode.

2. Launch Terminal in the directory in which you have your Podfile, type each of the lines that follow in order, press the Return key after each one, and wait for them to finish.

   ```
   sudo gem install cocoapods-deintegrate
   pod deintegrate
   pod install
   ```

The first line will install `deintegrate` on your system, which is a module of CocoaPods that removes any pods and all references to them from a project.

Skip this line if you already have `deintegrate` installed.

The second line will remove all pods from the project and clean any references to them.

The third line will install the same pods again.

3. Return to Xcode and select **Product ➤ Clean**.

4. Build the project again and you are done.

5. If necessary, restart Xcode.

Asset Catalogs Bug

Apple introduced Asset Catalogs on iOS 7 (Xcode 5). Using Asset Catalogs you can simplify management of images that your application uses as part of its user interface.

If you are a perfectionist, you will not like to hear about this Asset Catalogs bug that appears under the following circumstances:

1. Your project has two targets: one for iPhone and one for iPad.

2. Each target has a different icon.

3. You are compiling your project for iOS 7.

4. You have just one Assets Catalog file for all icons.

5. AppIcon is adjusted to have device-specific icons.

6. All icons are stored inside the AppIcon entry of Assets Catalog.

I am sorry to inform you, but this will not work as expected.

The bug

The iPhone target running on the iPad will show the iPad icon for iOS 7.x devices.

The solution

Create one Assets Catalog file with a different name for every platform you are supporting. Each Assets Catalog must contain its own AppIcon entry with a different name. Every AppIcon entry must contain just the icons belonging to the platform.

Don't forget to adjust each target to use the proper Assets Catalog and AppIcon entry.

App Crashing Without Giving You Clues?

The code presented in this section is specifically valuable if your Objective-C application is crashing with the infamous signal SIGABRT message and providing no other clues about the crash.

Replace the code on your **main.m** file with something like the following:

Objective-C

```
int main(int argc, char *argv[]) {
  int retVal;
  @autoreleasepool {
    @try {
      retVal = UIApplicationMain(argc, argv, nil, nil); //***
    }
    @catch (NSException *exception) {
      NSLog(@"\n\nSTACK SYMBOLS\n%@",  ↩
            [exception callStackSymbols]);
      NSLog(@"\n\nSTACK RETURN ADDRESSES\n%@",  ↩
            [exception callStackReturnAddresses]);
      NSLog(@"\n\nOBJECT: %@",[exception name]);
      NSLog(@"\n\nUSER INFO DICT: %@",[exception userInfo]);
      NSLog(@"\n\nREASON: %@",[exception reason]);
      retVal = 1;
    }
  }
  return retVal;
}
//*** this line should be typed like it is on your main.m.
```

In case of an application crash, this code will dump a lot of information to the console that may help you identify the problem.

> **Note**   Due to the nature of Swift, there is no way to implement this kind of code for that language.

NSUserDefaults Not Working for a Sandboxed App?

We have seen this problem a couple of times.

You are testing an application and suddenly it loses the ability to read or write to NSUserDefaults.

The typical solution for this problem is to restart your Mac, but everybody hates having to do that.

Instead, launch Terminal and type

```
ps auwx | grep cfprefsd | grep -v grep | awk '{print $2}' | ↵
xargs sudo kill -9
```

This will kill Mac OS X's cfprefsd daemon that provides preferences services for the CFPreferences and NSUserDefaults APIs (application programming interface).

The daemon will restart automatically the next time you try to access NSUserDefaults and everything should start working correctly.

Interface Elements Not Updating?

If you have an interface element like a spinner or a text view that must be updated constantly but the update is not happening because the application is busy on a loop, add the following code to the end of the loop.

Swift

```
var date : NSDate? = NSDate()
date = date!.dateByAddingTimeInterval(0.0)

let runLoop = NSRunLoop.currentRunLoop()
runLoop.runUntilDate(date!)
```

Objective-C

```
[[NSRunLoop currentRunLoop] runUntilDate:
            [NSDate dateWithTimeIntervalSinceNow:0.0]];
```

This code will force the loop to a brief pause and the application will be able to update the interface.

> **Note**   Bear in mind that this code will stop the current run loop for a fraction of time. This may slow down some apps. Use it with care. You can tweak the time interval if you want.

Find and Replace Strings Using Regex

Suppose your project contains multiple lines like the ones in this section.

Swift

```
myButton1.setTitleColor(UIColor.grayColor(), ↵
        forState:UIControlState.Normal)
myButton2.setTitleColor(UIColor. greenColor(), ↵
        forState:UIControlState.Selected)
myButton3.setTitleColor(UIColor. orangeColor(), ↵
        forState:UIControlState.Disabled)
```

Objective-C

```
[myButton1 setTitleColor:[UIColor grayColor] ↵
        forState: UIControlStateNormal];
[myButton2 setTitleColor:[UIColor greenColor] ↵
        forState: UIControlStateSelected];
[myButton3 setTitleColor:[UIColor orangeColor] ↵
        forState: UIControlStateDisabled];
```

The buttons have different names, different colors, and different control states.

You want to search for all lines like these and change the colors to red, but keep the names and the control states unchanged.

You want to change the code as shown next.

Swift

```
myButton1.setTitleColor(UIColor.redColor(), ↵
        forState:UIControlState.Normal)
myButton2.setTitleColor(UIColor.redColor(), ↵
        forState:UIControlState.Selected)
myButton3.setTitleColor(UIColor.redColor(), ↵
        forState:UIControlState.Disabled)
```

Objective-C

```
[myButton1 setTitleColor:[UIColor redColor] ↵
        forState: UIControlStateNormal];
[myButton2 setTitleColor:[UIColor redColor] ↵
        forState: UIControlStateSelected];
[myButton3 setTitleColor:[UIColor redColor] ↵
        forState: UIControlStateDisabled];
```

How do you do that?

Regular expressions will save you.

Using regular expressions

Note   Apple documentation says that when using regular expressions with Xcode's search we must use the ICU syntax. The ICU syntax uses the dollar ($) followed by a number to represent the capture group being referenced ($1, $2, etc.).

1.   Select **Find ➤ Find and Replace in Project....**

2.   Make sure you select **Replace** with the option **Regular Expression**. If not, click the **Text** word and select the proper option (see Figure 18 and Figure 19).

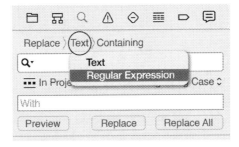

Figure 18. Regular expression option

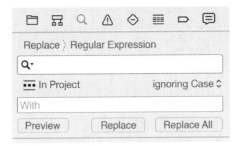

Figure 19. Regular expression selected

The Find field

The **Find** field is where you type the string or, in this case, the regular expression you want to find.

1. Fill the **Find** field with

   `\[(.*) setTitleColor:(.*) forState:(.*)\]`

Explanation:

You can divide this line into several parts (see Figure 20).

```
\[  (.*) setTitleColor:   (.*) forState:   (.*)   \]
❶   ❷                      ❸               ❹      ❺
```

Figure 20. Regular expression divided

❶ Find a left square bracket "[";

❷ Find anything that may exist between the left square bracket and setTitleColor: string and store what you find as "group 1";

❸ Find anything that may exist between setTitleColor: and forState: and store what you find as "group 2";

❹ Find anything that may exist between setTitleColor: and the right square bracket and store what you find as "group 3";

❺ Find a right square bracket "]";

> **Note**   The question here is, Why do we use the backslash before the bracket to search for the bracket? The answer is simple—because brackets are themselves part of the regular expression syntax. If we use an expression like [0-9] we tell Xcode to "find one number between 0 and 9." The backslash is there to tell Xcode that we want to find the bracket character, not to use the bracket as a command.
>
> The backslash character is what is known as the "escape" character, which according to Wikipedia is a character that invokes an alternative interpretation of subsequent characters in a character sequence.

The Replace field

The **Replace** field is where you type the expression you want to use to replace the text matching the **Find** field expression.

1. Fill the **Replace** field with

   [$1 setTitleColor:[UIColor redColor] forState:$3]

See Figure 21.

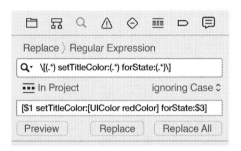

Figure 21. Regular expressions

Explanation

Variables **$1** and **$3** represent the capture groups of the **Find** field. As we said, "group 1" will be anything that may exist between the left square bracket and the setTitleColor: and "group 3" will be anything that may exist between setTitleColor: and the right square bracket. By using the variables **$1** and **$3** we are "pasting" in place the contents of "group 1" and "group 3."

In our example:

- ▓ "group 1" will contain different button names: myButton1, myButton2, and myButton3;

- ▓ "group 2" will contain the different colors: gray, green, and orange;

- ▓ "group 3" will contain different control states: normal, selected, and disabled.

By using the expression shown in the **Replace** field in Figure 21, we are instructing Xcode to build the replace string using the following method: start with a left square bracket, the contents of "group 1," a space, the string setTitleColor:[UIColor redColor] forState:, the contents of "group 3," and a right square bracket.

But there is the catch...

The search command we have described will work only if you type the lines continuously, as follows:

```
[myButton1 setTitleColor:...
                    forState:...];
```

If the lines are broken with line feeds, like the following ones, the search will not find them:

```
[myButton1 setTitleColor:...  ↵
                    forState:...];
```

The problem occurs because there is a line feed character (represented on this book by the ↵ character) between one part of the command and the other and we have not provided the search command with instructions to take that into account.

To account for line feeds or other invisible characters, you must add the **\s*** instruction to the search string.

In that case, the **Find** field changes to

```
\[(.*)\s*setTitleColor:(.*)\s*forState:(.*)\]
```

> **Note** The following characters are considered "blank characters" by the ICU syntax: tabs, form feeds, new lines, carriage returns, and any kind of spaces or invisible characters.
>
> You can find more about the ICU syntax by visiting `http://addfone.com/ TXICUSyntax`

Extracting a Dictionary from Array

You have an array of dictionaries and these dictionaries have two fields, "name" and "date," an NSString and an NSDate object, respectively.

At some point, you want to extract, from that array, the dictionary with the most recent date.

You can use a code like that shown here.

Swift: NSArray

```
// create the dictionaries with random dates
let obj1 : NSDictionary? = ["name":"car", ↵
                            "date":date1!]
let obj2 : NSDictionary? = ["name":"boat", ↵
                            "date":date2!]
let obj3 : NSDictionary? = ["name":"plane", ↵
                            "date":date3!]

// and store them on an array
let unsortedArray : NSArray = [obj1!, obj2!, obj3!]

// create a NSSortDescriptor to sort the array
let dateDescriptor : NSSortDescriptor = ↵
   NSSortDescriptor(key: "date", ascending: true)

// sorting the array
let sortedArrayOfDics : NSArray = ↵
   unsortedArray.sortedArrayUsingDescriptors([dateDescriptor])

// because the array is sorted, the last object is the
// one with the most recent date
let mostRecent : AnyObject! = sortedArrayOfDics.lastObject
```

A Swift variation...

The previous code works if you are dealing with an NSArray of NSDictionary objects, but what happens if you are working with a Swift array of Swift dictionaries?

In that case you must use the following code:

```
// creating the dictionaries
let dict1 : [String:AnyObject?] = ↵
           ["object" : "car",    "date" : date1]
let dict2 : [String:AnyObject?] = ↵
           ["object" : "boat",   "date" : date2]
```

```
let dict3 : [String:AnyObject?] = ↵
                          ["object ": "plane",  "date" : date3]

// creating the array
let array : Array = [dict1, dict2, dict3]

// creating the sort
let result = array.sort {
  item1, item2 in
  let date1 = item1["date"] as! NSDate
  let date2 = item2["date"] as! NSDate
  return date1.compare(date2) == ↵
                       NSComparisonResult.OrderedAscending
}
let latestDate = result.last
print(latestDate)
```

Objective-C

```
// the dictionaries with random dates
NSDictionary *obj1 = @{ @"name":@"car", ↵
                       @"date":date1};
NSDictionary *obj2 = @{ @"name":@"boat", ↵
                       @"date":date2};
NSDictionary *obj3 = @{ @"name":@"plane", ↵
                       @"date":date3};
// the unsorted array
NSArray *unsortedArray = @[obj1, obj2, obj3];

// create a NSSortDescriptor to sort the array
NSSortDescriptor *dateDescriptor = [NSSortDescriptor ↵
             sortDescriptorWithKey:@"date" ascending:YES];

NSArray *sortDescriptors = @[dateDescriptor];

// sorting the array
NSArray *sortedArray = [unsortedArray ↵
             sortedArrayUsingDescriptors:sortDescriptors];

// because the array is sorted, the last object is the
// one with the most recent date
NSDictionary *mostRecent = [sortedArray lastObject];
```

Magical Way for Counting Elements in Arrays

Suppose you have an array of dictionaries and these dictionaries have two fields, "object" and "selected," an NSString and a BOOL stored as an NSNumber, respectively.

You want to know how many of these dictionaries have the selected field equal to YES/true.

The first code that comes to mind is shown next.

Swift

```
var count = 0
for dict in array {
  if dict["selected"] == true
     count++
}
```

Objective-C

```
NSInteger count = 0;
for (NSDictionary * dict in array) {
  BOOL isSelected = [dict [@"selected"] boolValue];
  if (isSelected)
    count++;
}
```

But this code is not magical.

Let's do it the magical way.

Swift: NSArray

```
// creating the dictionaries
let dict1: NSDictionary = ["object"   : "television",
                           "selected" : true]
let dict2: NSDictionary = ["object"   : "phone",
                           "selected" : false]
let dict3: NSDictionary = ["object"   : "book",
                           "selected" : true]

// creating the array
let array : NSArray? = [dict1, dict2, dict3]
```

```
// this is the magical command
let count = ↵
            array!.valueForKeyPath("@sum.selected")?.integerValue

print(count); // this will print 2 on console
```

A Swift variation...

The previous code will only work if you are using a NSArray of
NSDictionaries. If you are using a Swift array of Swift dictionaries you
should use the following code:

```
// creating the dictionaries
let dict1 = ["object" : "television", "selected": true]
let dict2 = ["object" : "phone",      "selected": false]
let dict3 = ["object" : "book",       "selected": true]

// creating the array
let array = [dict1, dict2, dict3]

// the magic command
let filteredArray = array.filter({$0["selected"] == true})

let result = filteredArray.count
print(result) // this will print 2 on console
```

Objective-C

```
// creating the dictionaries
NSDictionary *dict1 = @{@"object"    : @"television",
                        @"selected"  : @(YES) };
NSDictionary *dict2 = @{@"object"    : @"phone",
                        @"selected"  : @(NO)  };
NSDictionary *dict3 = @{@"object"    : @"book",
                        @"selected"  : @(YES) };

// creating the array
NSArray *array = @[dict1, dict2, dict3];

// this is the magical command
NSInteger count = [[array ↵
                        valueForKeyPath:@"@sum.selected"] integerValue];

NSLog(@"count %@", @(count)); // this will print 2 on console
```

OS X App Not Launching with the Correct Size

If you have adjusted your Cocoa application to launch with a certain size but the app is failing to do so, this section is definitely for you.

We have seen this problem more than once, and it is usually related to some Auto Layout constraint that is interfering with the initial ViewController.

The solution for this problem would be to apply constraints to the ViewController's view, making it launch with the correct size, but these kinds of views do not accept constraints.

You have to embed the whole interface into an NSView and apply constraints to that view, defining the size you want your application to launch (Figure 22).

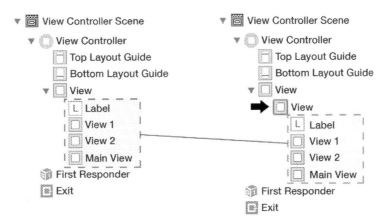

Figure 22. Embedding the whole interface elements into a view (before and after)

Detecting the Application Target Running

You have a project with independent iPhone and iPad targets and at some point in the code you want to know what target is running.

Using UI_USER_INTERFACE_IDIOM() is not an option because this method will just check if the target is running on iPhone or iPad, not the target itself.

One way to solve this problem involves adding a preprocessor macro and testing for the existence of that macro later in code, but compiler directives make the code clumsy and reduce readability.

However, there is a better way. The code shown next will read the bundle's infoDictionary and discover which target is running.

Swift

```
func getTarget() -> NSString {

  let dict : NSDictionary = ↩
              NSBundle.mainBundle().infoDictionary!

  let family  = dict["UIDeviceFamily"]!
  let device = family[0]

  return (device.integerValue == 1) ? "iPhone" : "iPad"
}
```

Objective-C

```
- (NSString *) getTarget {

  NSDictionary *dict = [[NSBundle mainBundle] infoDictionary];
  NSArray *family = dict[@"UIDeviceFamily"];
  NSInteger device = [family[0] integerValue];

  return (device == 1) ? @"iPhone" : @"iPad";
}
```

Disabling a Method on a Class

You have a new class that has to be initialized using a specific method such as initWithMode: and you want to prevent people from using other initialization methods that the superclass may provide.

The code shown next will warn people to use the correct initialization method and disable other methods that may exist.

Swift

```
@available(*, unavailable, ↵
          message="init is unavailable, use initWithMode")
init() {
  // your code...
}
```

Objective-C

```
#import <Foundation/Foundation.h>

@interface SampleClass : NSObject

- (id)init __attribute__((unavailable("init is unavailable, ↵
                      use initWithMode")));
@end
```

> **Note** This directive will produce an error at compile time, warning users that they should not be using the init method for initialization.

Deprecating a Method on a Class

You have deprecated a method on a class and you want to warn your users to update their codes to use the new method.

You can simply add this compiler attribute to the method.

Swift

```
@available(*, deprecated)
class func shareWithParams(params: NSDictionary) {
  // your code...
}
```

Objective-C

```
#import <Foundation/Foundation.h>

@interface SampleClass : NSObject

+(void)shareWithParams:(NSDictionary *)params ↵
      __attribute((deprecated("use shareWithPars: ↵
      instead")));
@end
```

> **Note**   This compiler attribute will produce an error at compile time, warning that the current method is deprecated and that another one should be used.

Xcode "Beachballing" on You

Is Xcode "beachballing" forever on you when we try to open a project that was working fine the day before?

> **Note**   The Spinning Beach Ball of Death or spinning wait cursor is a colorful round cursor type, resembling a beach ball, that replaces the regular mouse pointer when an application hangs on Mac OS X.

It turns out that disabling **Source Control** in Xcode **Preferences** solves the issue (Figure 23).

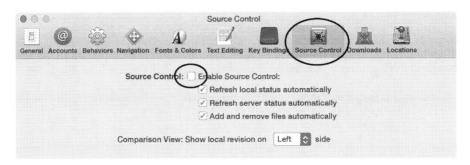

Figure 23. "Beachballing" problem solved by disabling Source Control

> **Note**   The Source Control problem described here is also responsible for making Xcode crash when you try to open some projects.

UIButton Not Grayed-Out

You are trying to disable a UIButton by using the following code but the button is not grayed-out.

Swift

```
myButton.enabled = false
```

Objective-C

```
myButton.enabled = NO;
```

UIButton objects are not displayed as grayed-out when they are disabled. You have to force a gray color on their titles to make them appear "disabled" by using the code shown next.

Swift

```
myButton.enabled = false
myButton.setTitleColor(UIColor.grayColor(), ↵
                    forState:UIControlState.Disabled)
```

Objective-C

```
myButton.enabled = NO;
[myButton setTitleColor:[UIColor grayColor] ↵
                    forState:UIControlStateDisabled];
```

Catching Memory Corruption

Some kinds of bugs are simply hard to catch.

Your application crashes and the situation is odd and difficult to track down.

Your users start yelling and you cannot reproduce the problem.

Your application is probably facing some kind of memory corruption.

This is what Apple has to say about it.

> *Objective-C and C code are susceptible to memory corruption issues such as stack and heap buffer overruns and use-after-free issues. When these memory violations occur, your app can crash unpredictably or display odd behavior. Memory corruption issues are difficult to track down because the crashes and odd behavior are often hard to reproduce and the cause can be far from the origin of the problem.*

For more information, visit `http://addfone.com/TXSanitizer`

The Sanitizer

Xcode 7 comes with an option called **Address Sanitizer** that generates extra code in the application to check every read and write through a pointer, warning if some address in memory gets corrupted.

To enable this option, select **Product ➤ Scheme ➤ Edit Scheme ➤ Diagnostics** and select **Enable Address Sanitizer** (Figure 24).

Figure 24. Xcode 7 Address Sanitizer

Run your application after enabling **Address Sanitizer** until it crashes. Crashes will now produce juicy error messages that will give you clues about the problem.

Your users will stop yelling.

> **Note**   Address Sanitizer may impose a substantial overhead and slow down your code to at least half the normal speed.

SpriteKit Crashing on didBeginContact

spritekit Assertion failed: (typeA == b2_dynamicBody || typeB == b2_dynamicBody), function SolveTOI

SpriteKit's didBeginContact: method is called every time two objects collide. While this method is running, SpriteKit expects that at least one of the colliding objects is dynamic (physicsBody.dynamic = YES). If one of the objects changes from dynamic to static while didBeginContact: is running, SpriteKit will crash.

One of the workarounds to prevent the crash is to manipulate a temporary variable instead of the dynamic property itself. See the code shown next.

Swift

```
let tempBody = self.physicsBody
tempBody!.dynamic = false
self.physicsBody = tempBody
```

Objective-C

```
SKPhysicsBody *tempBody = node.physicsBody;
tempBody.dynamic = NO;
node.physicsBody = tempBody;
```

> **Note**   This solution must be used just to confirm the problem. You must check your code and prevent it from changing the properties of both physicsBody to static during didBeginContact:
>
> This solution does not work correctly if your physicsBody belongs to a node that was scaled up or down. In this case, when you assign the tempBody back to the object, it will create a physicsBody that is not scaled.

SpriteKit Object Is Not Respecting Boundaries?

You have SpriteKit objects using paths as their physicsBody boundaries, but these objects are not respecting the edges/boundaries of other objects.

All paths used by SpriteKit objects should be convex and created with vertices drawn in counter-clockwise order (Figure 25).

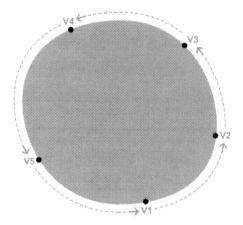

Figure 25. Convex shape drawn in the correct order

Verify if your paths are following this rule or if any shape created with them is non-convex (Figure 26).

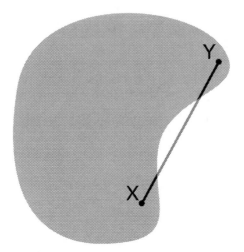

Figure 26. *Non-convex shape; order of vertices doesn't matter*

Note   You can detect if a shape is non-convex by drawing a line between two points inside the shape. If the connecting line falls outside the shape it is non-convex. SpriteKit objects must be convex (Figure 25) created with vertices drawn in counter-clockwise order.

A Case Against Using Storyboards for Cocoa Apps

This is a deadly combination:

1. You are creating a Cocoa application.

2. Your application needs to load and save files using [NSPanel openPanel] and [NSPanel savePanel], respectively.

3. You create the application using storyboard.

4. You choose to require OS X 10.10.0 as the minimum OS required for the application.

We are sorry to inform you that your application **will not work**.

The reason is a bug on OS X 10.10.0 and 10.10.1 that doesn't just prevent [NSPanel openPanel] and [NSPanel savePanel] from working but indeed makes the application crash if you try to use these methods.

This code, for example, crashes in OS X 10.10.0 and 10.10.1 but works perfectly in 10.10.2 and up.

Swift

```
let panel  = NSSavePanel()
panel.beginSheetModalForWindow(self.view.window!, ↵
            completionHandler: { (result) -> Void in
})
```

Objective-C

```
NSSavePanel*  panel = [NSSavePanel savePanel];

panel beginSheetModalForWindow:self.view.window ↵
            completionHandler:^(NSInteger result){
}];
```

Following is the answer we received from Apple, after contacting them about the problem:

> *Our engineers have reviewed your request and have determined that you are experiencing a known issue, the workaround for which is to* **replace storyboards with xibs***.*
>
> *Alternatively, you may choose to require OS X 10.10.2 as the minimum OS for this app.*

The problem with storyboards for OS X applications don't end with the NSSavePanel and NSOpenPanel. Neither will NSSplitControllers and NSTabViewControllers work well with storyboards, under certain circumstances.

So, until OS X 10.10 is history, we recommend not using storyboards for your OS X projects. Use XIBs as recommended by Apple.

UIView Classes with Independent Rounded Corners

> **Note** UIButton, UILabel, UISegmentedControl, and UITextView are some examples of UIView-based classes.

If you want to create rounded-corner UIView base classes and have the ability to control the radius of every corner independently, we have created this category ("extension" in Swift) for you.

Swift

UIView+IndependentCorners.swift

```
import UIKit
import QuartzCore

extension UIView {

  func corners(corners: UIRectCorner, radius : CGFloat){
    let maskPath = UIBezierPath(roundedRect: bounds, ↵
                            byRoundingCorners: corners, cornerRadii: ↵
        CGSizeMake(radius, radius))

    let cornerLayer = CAShapeLayer()
    cornerLayer.frame = self.bounds
    cornerLayer.path = maskPath.CGPath
    layer.mask = cornerLayer
  }
}
```

Set the corners by using the following code:

```
// set the radius of both, the top left and
// the bottom right corners to 20 pt
myVIew.corners(UIRectCorner.TopLeft | ↵
                                UIRectCorner.BottomRight, radius: 20)
```

> **Note**   You can combine multiple corners by separating them with a pipe
> character ("|"). The options are UIRectCorner.TopLeft, UIRectCorner.
> TopRight, UIRectCorner.BottomLeft, UIRectCorner.BottomRight,
> and UIRectCorner.AllCorners.

Objective-C

UIView+IndependentCorners.h

```objectivec
#import <UIKit/UIKit.h>

@interface UIView (IndependentCorners)

- (void)setCorners:(UIRectCorner)corners ↵
                   withRadius:(CGFloat)radius;

@end
```

UIView+IndependentCorners.m

```objectivec
#import "UIView+ IndependentCorners.h"

@implementation UIView (IndependentCorners)

- (void)setCorners:(UIRectCorner)corners ↵
                                withRadius:(CGFloat)radius
{
  UIBezierPath *shapePath = [UIBezierPath ↵
                                bezierPathWithRoundedRect:[self bounds] ↵
                byRoundingCorners:corners ↵
                        cornerRadii:CGSizeMake(radius, radius];

  CAShapeLayer *newCornerLayer = [CAShapeLayer layer];
  newCornerLayer.frame = [self bounds];
  newCornerLayer.path = shapePath.CGPath;
  [self layer].mask = newCornerLayer;
}

@end
```

Set the corners by using the following code:

```
// set the radius of both, the top left and
// the bottom right corners to 30 pt

[myView setMaskTo:self.pickerFrom ↵
        byRoundingCorners:UIRectCornerBottomLeft | ↵
                              UIRectCornerBottomRight ↵
          withCornerRadii:CGSizeMake(30.0f, 30.0f)];
```

> **Note** Like the Swift example, you can combine multiple corners by separating them with a pipe character ("|"). The options are UIRectCornerTopLeft, UIRectCornerTopRight, UIRectCornerBottomLeft, UIRectCornerBottomRight, and UIRectCornerAllCorners.

Making NSViews "Compatible" with UIViews

If you create iOS and OS X applications, you have certainly wished you could use the code you previously created for one platform for the other. One of most classic cases involves UIViews and NSViews.

The problem with UIViews and NSViews is that they are different animals. At the end of the day, you have to create different codes for both classes even if you are doing the same simple operations with them.

While we agree that UIViews and NSViews are different animals, we also see that they have a lot in common. It doesn't make sense to have different commands for the same functionality like setAlpha: and setAlphaValue: to set the view's transparency on iOS and OS X, respectively.

We have created a class for you, to make UIView and NSView objects similar for some simple aspects. This class also adds some power functionality to NSViews, like the ability to fade in and out of these views and to set the view's position by its center.

Swift

NSView+ CompatibleUIView.swift

```swift
import Foundation
import AppKit

extension NSView {

    typealias AnimationHandler  = () -> Void
    typealias CompletionHandler = (finished : Bool) -> Void

    var center:CGPoint {
        get {
            let midX = CGRectGetMidX(frame)
            let midY = CGRectGetMidY(frame)
            return CGPointMake(midX, midY)
        }
        set(newCenter) {
            var newFrame = CGRectZero
            newFrame.size = frame.size

            let myWidth = CGRectGetWidth(frame)
            let myHeight = CGRectGetHeight(frame)

            let x = floor(newCenter.x - (myWidth / 2.0) )
            let y = floor(newCenter.y - (myHeight / 2.0) )
```

```
    newFrame.origin.x = x
    newFrame.origin.y = y

    frame = newFrame
  }
}

var alpha : CGFloat {
    get{ return alphaValue }
    set(value) { alphaValue = value }
}

func fadeInWithDuration (duration : NSTimeInterval) {
    wantsLayer = true
    NSAnimationContext.beginGrouping()
    NSAnimationContext.currentContext().duration = ↵
                                        duration
    animator().alphaValue = 1.0
    NSAnimationContext.endGrouping()
}

func fadeOutWithDuration (duration : NSTimeInterval) {
    wantsLayer = true
    NSAnimationContext.beginGrouping()
    NSAnimationContext.currentContext().duration = ↵
                                                duration
    animator().alphaValue = 0.0
    NSAnimationContext.endGrouping()
}
func animateWithDuration (duration : NSTimeInterval, ↵
                    animations:AnimationHandler) {
        wantsLayer = true
        NSAnimationContext.runAnimationGroup({↵
                (context: NSAnimationContext) -> Void in

        context.duration = duration
        context.allowsImplicitAnimation = true

        animations()
        }, completionHandler: { () -> Void in  })
}
func animateWithDuration (duration : NSTimeInterval, ↵
                    animations:AnimationHandler, ↵
    completion:CompletionHandler) {
            wantsLayer = true
```

```
NSAnimationContext.runAnimationGroup({ ↵
                    (context: NSAnimationContext) -> Void in

context.duration = duration
context.allowsImplicitAnimation = true

animations()
}, completionHandler: { () -> Void in ↵
    completion(finished:true)
})
  }
}
```

This category will make it possible to use setAlpha: and setCenter: with your NSViews and, as a bonus, add some powerful functionalities to them.

Fade in and fade out

```
// fade in or fade out myView in 5 seconds
myView.fadeInWithDuration(5)
myView.fadeOutWithDuration(5)
```

Animating a NSView just like a UIView

```
// animate myView's alpha from 0 to 0.7 in 5 seconds
myView.alpha = 0
myView.animateWithDuration(5.0, animations: { () -> Void in
    self.myView.alphaValue = 0.7
})

// or

// animate myView's alpha from 0 to 0.7 in 5 seconds
// and do something when the animation finishes
self.myView.animateWithDuration(5.0,
  animations: { () -> Void in
      self.myView.alphaValue = 0.7
  }, completion: { (finished) -> Void in
    // animation finished... do something here
})
```

Objective-C

NSView+ CompatibleUIView.h

```
@class NSView;

@interface NSView (CompatibleUIView)

- (void)setAlpha:(CGFloat)point;
- (CGFloat)alpha;
- (void)setCenter:(CGPoint)point;
- (CGPoint)center;

+(void)fadeOut:(NSView*)viewToDissolve ↲
  withDuration:(NSTimeInterval)duration;

+(void)fadeIn:(NSView*)viewToFadeIn ↲
 withDuration:(NSTimeInterval)duration;

+ (void)animateWithDuration:(NSTimeInterval)duration ↲
               animations:(void (^)(void))animations;

+ (void)animateWithDuration:(NSTimeInterval)duration ↲
               animations:(void (^)(void))animations ↲
               completion:(void (^)(BOOL
                                  finished))completion;
@end
```

NSView+ CompatibleUIView.m

```
#import "NSView+CompatibleUIView.h"
#import <Cocoa/Cocoa.h>

@implementation NSView (CompatibleUIView)

- (void)setAlpha:(CGFloat)point {
  [self setAlphaValue:point];
}

- (CGFloat)alpha {
  return self.alphaValue;
}

- (void)setCenter:(CGPoint)point {
  CGSize size = self.frame.size;
  CGRect newFrame = CGRectZero;
  newFrame.size = size;
```

```
  CGFloat width = CGRectGetWidth(self.frame);
  CGFloat height = CGRectGetHeight(self.frame);

  CGFloat x = floorf(point.x - (width / 2.0f));
  CGFloat y = floorf(point.y - (height / 2.0f));

  newFrame.origin.x = x;
  newFrame.origin.y = y;

  [self setFrame:newFrame];
}
- (CGPoint)center {
  return CGPointMake(CGRectGetMidX(self.frame),
                     CGRectGetMidY(self.frame));
}


+(void)fadeOut:(NSView*)viewToDissolve
  withDuration:(NSTimeInterval)duration
{
  [NSAnimationContext beginGrouping];
  [[NSAnimationContext currentContext] setDuration:duration];
  [[viewToDissolve animator] setAlphaValue:0.0];
  [NSAnimationContext endGrouping];
}

+(void)fadeIn:(NSView*)viewToFadeIn
 withDuration:(NSTimeInterval)duration
{
  [NSAnimationContext beginGrouping];
  [[NSAnimationContext currentContext] setDuration:duration];
  [[viewToFadeIn animator] setAlphaValue:1.0f];
  [NSAnimationContext endGrouping];
}

+ (void)animateWithDuration:(NSTimeInterval)duration
               animations:(void (^)(void))animations
{
  [NSAnimationContext beginGrouping];
  [[NSAnimationContext currentContext] setDuration:duration];
  animations();
  [NSAnimationContext endGrouping];
}

+ (void)animateWithDuration:(NSTimeInterval)duration
               animations:(void (^)(void))animations
               completion:(void (^)(BOOL finished))completion
```

```
{
  [NSAnimationContext beginGrouping];
  [[NSAnimationContext currentContext] setDuration:duration];
  animations();
  [NSAnimationContext endGrouping];

  if(animations)
  {
    id completionBlock = [completion copy];
    [self performSelector:@selector(runEndBlock:)
              withObject:completionBlock
              afterDelay:duration];
  }
}

+ (void)runEndBlock:(void (^)(void))completionBlock
{
  completionBlock();
}

@end
```

The following code shows you how to use the powerful functionalities:

Fade in and fade out

```
[NSView fadeIn:myView withDuration:1.0];
[NSView fadeOut:myView withDuration:1.0];
```

Animating a NSView just like a UIView

```
[NSView animateWithDuration:1.0 animations:^{
  [myView setAlphaValue:0.7f];
}
```

```
// or
```

```
[NSView animateWithDuration:1.0 animations:^{
  [myView setAlpha:0.7f];

} completion:^(BOOL finished) {
  // do something after the animation finishes
}];
```

Detect when the UIPickerView Stops Spinning

UIPickerView doesn't have a direct way for detecting when its wheels stop spinning, but we can use a trick to detect that.

First, locate, in your code, the line that puts the wheels in motion and add the code shown next.

Swift

```
UIView.beginAnimations("animation", context: nil)
UIPickerView.setAnimationDelegate(self)
UIView.setAnimationDidStopSelector( Selector("animationDidStop:finished:
context:") )

// this is the line that puts the wheels in motion
picker.selectRow(value, inComponent: 0, animated: true)

UIView.commitAnimations()
```

This code will run when the wheels stop spinning:

```
func animationDidStop(animationID: String?, ↵
        finished: NSNumber, context: UnsafeMutablePointer<Void>) {
  print( "animation finished!" )
}
```

Objective-C

```
[UIView beginAnimations:@"animation" context:nil];
[UIPickerView setAnimationDelegate:self];

[UIPickerView setAnimationDidStopSelector: ↵
                        @selector(animationFinished:finished:context:)];

// this is the line that puts the wheels in motion
[self selectRow:value inComponent:0 animated:YES];

[UIView commitAnimations];
```

This code will run when the wheels stop spinning:

```
- (void) animationFinished:(NSString *)animationID ↵
        finished:(BOOL)finished context:(void *)context {
  NSLog(@"animation finished");
}
```

"Insane" NSDates

Next is the code for creating a NSDate.

Swift

```
let comps    = NSDateComponents()
comps.day   = 22
comps.month = 8
comps.year   = 2020

let gregorian = NSCalendar(identifier: ↵
          NSCalendarIdentifierGregorian)

let date = gregorian?.dateFromComponents(comps)

print("Date is " , date)
```

Objective-C

```
NSDateComponents *comps = [[NSDateComponents alloc] init];
[comps setDay:22];
[comps setMonth:8];
[comps setYear:2020];

NSCalendar *gregorian = [[NSCalendar alloc] ↵
              initWithCalendarIdentifier: ↵
          NSCalendarIdentifierGregorian];

NSDate *date = [gregorian dateFromComponents:comps];

NSLog(@"Date is %@", date);
```

The date is August 22, 2020, right? However, when you look at the console you see

Date is 2020-08-21 23:00:00 +0000

What?!! August 21, 2020???!!

The problem is that both NSLog and print use the UTC (coordinated universal time) date representation that takes time zones into account.

If you need to create a date that does not take time zones into account, or, in better words, a date that uses a time zone reference as "default," add one extra line to your code (shown in **bold**), after creating the Gregorian variable.

The code will be converted to

Swift

```
let comps    = NSDateComponents()
comps.day    = 22
comps.month = 8
comps.year   = 2020

let gregorian = NSCalendar(identifier: ↵
            NSCalendarIdentifierGregorian)

// the magical line
gregorian?.timeZone = NSTimeZone(forSecondsFromGMT: 0)

let date = gregorian?.dateFromComponents(comps)

print("Date is " , date)
```

Objective-C

```
NSDateComponents *comps = [[NSDateComponents alloc] init];
[comps setDay:22];
[comps setMonth:8];
[comps setYear:2020];

NSCalendar *gregorian = [[NSCalendar alloc] ↵
                initWithCalendarIdentifier: ↵
      NSCalendarIdentifierGregorian];

// the magical line
gregorian.timeZone = [NSTimeZone timeZoneForSecondsFromGMT:0];

NSDate *date = [gregorian dateFromComponents:comps];

NSLog(@"Date is %@", date);
```

Now the result will be

Date is 2020-08-22 00:00:00 +0000

Localizing the Application Name

If you want your iOS or OS X applications to have different names in the different countries in which they are sold, you can localize the name by using a special kind of file called `InfoPlist.strings`.

Just follow these steps:

1. Select **File ➤ New ➤ File ➤** choose **iOS** or **OS X ➤ Resource ➤ Strings File**, create a file named `InfoPlist.strings` and assign this file to the desired target.

2. Add the following keys to `InfoPlist.strings`:

   ```
   "CFBundleDisplayName" = "AAA";
   "CFBundleName" = "BBB";
   ```

   Replace **AAA** and **BBB** with the application's name and the bundle name on a particular language, respectively.

3. Localize `InfoPlist.strings` to the languages you need.

Note   You may have noticed that `InfoPlist.strings` contain the keys `CFBundleDisplayName` and `CFBundleName` that are also present on `Info.plist`. The keys on `InfoPlist.strings` will have priority over their equivalents on `Info.plist`.

Centering Views Horizontally with Auto Layout

WARNING! You are now entering the heart of the beast, a dangerous territory from which no one has ever come back sane. From now on, all your fights will be epic ones, against creatures that have no mercy.

Forget about logical thinking and welcome to Auto Layout.

Example

You have three simple views. All views have the same width and height and are equally spaced (Figure 27). Your objective is to use Auto Layout and make the views appear exactly like the one in Figure 27 across all devices.

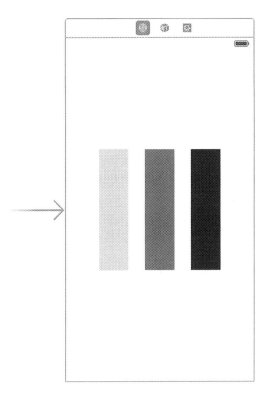

Figure 27. Three aligned views

Oops... bad idea

The first idea to make these views look like the one in Figure 27 across devices is to let Xcode create the constraints for you. For that, select the storyboard file on Xcode's Project Navigator and click **Editor ➤Resolve Auto Layout Issues ➤ Reset to Suggested Constraints**. The result of this action across devices is what you see in Figure 28.

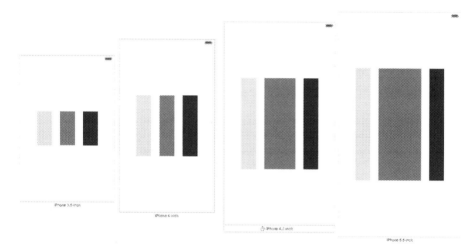

Figure 28. Result from Auto Layout

What?!

Then you think: the problem is that we have to constrain the views to have the "same width," the "same height," and the same "aspect ratio." Nope, if you do that, the result is as wrong as the first one.

Then you try another approach. You define constraints for the "width" and "height" of those views and to the spacing between them. No way, Jose! The result is even worse.

Several tries later, you give up. No logical or intuitive thinking can save you.

You are now alone in the jungle and the beast is watching you.

Logic just left the room

Following is how you solve this problem, using what appears to be a kind of "hack," which apparently is the accepted way of solving things in Auto Layout:

1. Select all views.

2. Click the **Pin** button at the bottom of the Interface Builder panel and select **Equal Widths, Equal Heights**, and **Aspect Ratio** and click **Add 6 Constraints**. That will make all three views have the same width, height, and aspect ratio (see Figure 29).

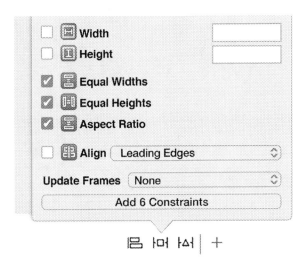

Figure 29. Width, Height, and Aspect Ratio

3. Select the first view only, return to the **Pin** menu, select **Width** and **Height**, and click **Add 2 Constraints** (see Figure 30). This will define the width and height of the first view. The other views will have the same size because of the constraints you have added on the previous step.

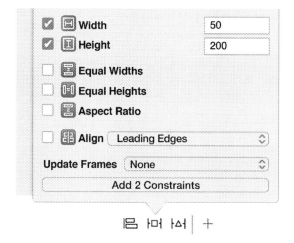

Figure 30. Width/height of the first view

4. Select all views, click the **Alignment** Button on the bottom of Interface Builder Panel, select **Horizontal Center in Container**, **Vertical Center in Container**, and **Add 6 Constraints** (see Figure 31).

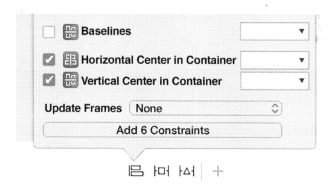

Figure 31. Horizontal and vertical centers

Note   In step 4 we have added a **Horizontal Center in Container** constraint to all views. By adding this, we are telling Auto Layout to align all three views at the horizontal container center, which is illogical, because this is not where we want the views to be. The next step will solve the problem.

This is how you defeat the beast

1. Select **Editor ➤ Resolve Auto Layout Issues ➤ Update Constraints**. This step adds a horizontal offset to all views, solving the problem caused by the last step. In other words, each view will be located "at the horizontal center plus an offset."

Figure 32 shows the final result.

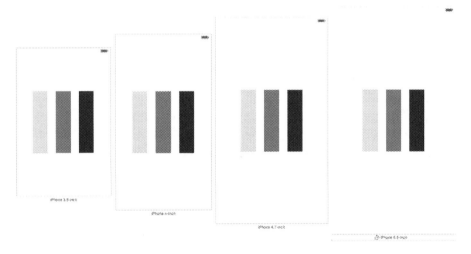

Figure 32. Final result Auto Layout

All views are the same size and have the same spacing across devices.

Elements Grayed-Out on Storyboard After Copying

You have copied a view controller or its elements between storyboards or projects and after finishing copying you notice that some of these elements are grayed-out (Figure 33). Why?

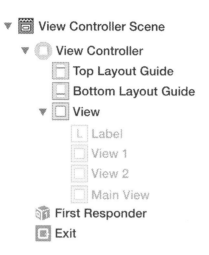

Figure 33. Elements grayed out on storyboard

The problem occurred because you have copied elements between storyboards with different Size Classes.

See the Size Classes selection button in Figure 34.

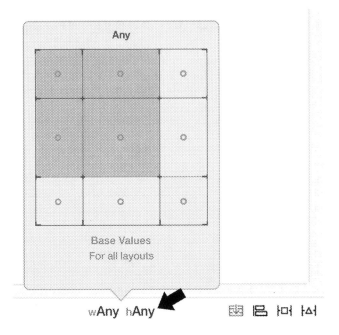

Figure 34. *Size Class selection*

If you copy an element from a storyboard that is adjusted as Any/Any to another one that is not adjusted like that, this element will be grayed out.

The Size Classes selection must be the same for both storyboards or the elements will be grayed-out after copying.

To solve that problem, follow these steps:

1. Make a copy of the storyboard you will copy the elements from.

2. Disable **Size Classes** for that storyboard by unchecking the correspondent box (see Figure 35).

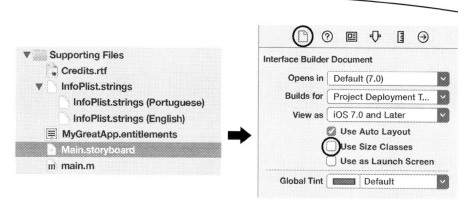

Figure 35. Use Size Classes option

3.   Copy the desired interface elements from this copied storyboard to the final one.

Elements will no longer be grayed-out after copying.

Debugging Core Data

When you deal with a database-intensive application using Core Data, many operations happen under the hood to keep the juices flowing.

When something strange happens during one of these operations, the application will crash and it will probably be very difficult to discover the problem.

In the section "Concurrency with Core Data," we described one of the issues that can affect Core Data applications, but other obscure problems can crop up.

Alone in the dark

If the problem is strange and obscure, you can enable Xcode's ability to debug Core Data operations by selecting **Product ➤ Scheme ➤ Edit ➤ Scheme ➤ Arguments** and adding the key-com.apple.CoreData.SQLDebug 3 to the **Arguments Passed on Launch** section (Figure 36).

Figure 36. Debugging Core Data

> **Note**   The option -com.apple.CoreData.SQLDebug takes a value between 1 and 3. Higher values increase the verbosity level.

Once this key is turned on, Xcode's log displays information like that shown in Figure 37.

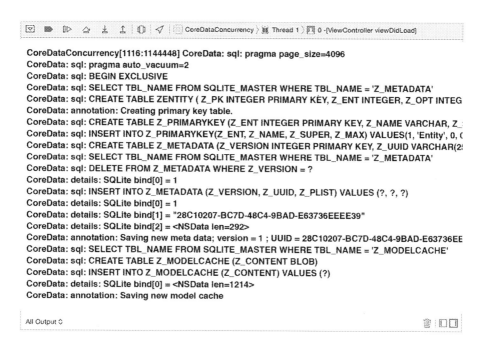

Figure 37. *Core Data debug information*

The package does not contain an Info.plist

This error message generally appears when you try to validate or submit your application to the App Store.

This message tells you that the Info.plist file is missing. In fact, the message is misleading because this error message can appear also if some keys are missing from your Info.plist file.

The following keys will trigger the error if they are missing from the Info.plist file: CFBundleVersion, CFBundleShortVersionString, and CFBundlePackageType.

- **CFBundleVersion.** This key specifies the build version number for the bundle.

- **CFBundleShortVersionString.** This key stores the release-version-number string for the bundle.

- **CFBundlePackageType.** This key usually contains a four-letter code identifying the bundle type. The possible values are

  - **APPL** – the package is an application;

  - **FMWK** – the package is a framework;

  - **BNDL** – the package is a loadable bundle.

Note   iOS and OS X applications use all these keys.

For more information, visit http://www.addfone.com/TXCFKeys

To check if your Info.plist file has any of these keys missing, open your target's **Info** panel, right-click any of the keys, and choose **Show Raw Keys/Value** (Figure 38).

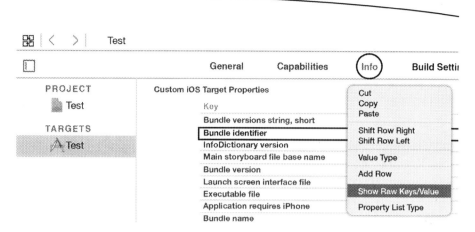

Figure 38. Info.plist keys (friendly names)

After selecting this option, the keys will not be displayed with their friendly names, as in Figure 38. Instead, they will be displayed using their unfriendly Core Foundation (CF) names (Figure 39), exactly what you need.

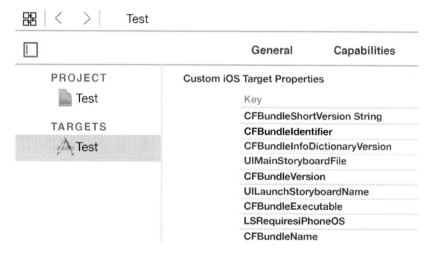

Figure 39. Info.plist keys (CF names)

Check the Version of an App in the App Store

If for some reason you need to check the version of your iOS or OS X application in the App Store, use the code shown next.

Swift

```
func getAppVersion ( onCompletion: (version: String) -> Void) {

    // get the app's bundle identifier
    let bundleIdentifier = "com.yourCompany.yourAppBundleID"

    // build the app path using iTunes API
    let path : String = "http://itunes.apple.com/↵
                              lookup?bundleId=\(bundleIdentifier)"

    let lookupURL : NSURL = NSURL(string:path)!
    let session = NSURLSession.sharedSession()

    let request = NSURLRequest(URL: lookupURL)

    // request data about the application, asynchronously
    // using iTunes API
    let task = session.dataTaskWithRequest(request, ↵
                        completionHandler: { data, response, error in

        if !(error != nil) {
        do {
        let jsonResults = try ↵
                        NSJSONSerialization.JSONObjectWithData(data!, ↵
                            options: []) as! NSDictionary
        let results = jsonResults["results"]
        let appDetails = results?.firstObject

        // get the application version
        let latestVersion = appDetails!!["version"] as! String
        onCompletion(version: latestVersion)
    }
        catch let error as NSError {
        print("error = \(error)")
    }
        catch {   }
        }
        })

    task.resume()

}
```

You must use it like this

```
getAppVersion { (version) -> Void in
  print("latest version = ", version)
}
```

Objective-C

```
-(void)getAppVersionAndRunOnCompletion: ↩
        (void (^)(NSString *version))completionBlock {

  // get the app's bundle identifier
  NSString *bundleIdentifier = ↩
                      @"com.yourCompany.yourAppBundleID";

  // use iTunes API to get data about the application
  NSURL *lookupURL = [NSURL URLWithString:[NSString ↩
                        stringWithFormat: @"http://itunes.apple.com/ ↩
          lookup?bundleId=%@", bundleIdentifier]];

  NSURLSession *session = [NSURLSession sharedSession];
  [[session dataTaskWithURL:lookupURL ↩
          completionHandler:^(NSData *data,↩
                            NSURLResponse *response, ↩
                            NSError *error) {

          // data is nil or error occurred, exit with nil
          if ( (data == nil) || (error != nil) ) {
            completionBlock(nil);
            return;
          }

          NSDictionary *jsonResults = [NSJSONSerialization ↩
                        JSONObjectWithData:data options:0 ↩
                                            error:nil];

          NSUInteger resultCount = [[jsonResults ↩
                        objectForKey: @"resultCount"] ↩
                                            integerValue];
```

```
            // number of objects on jsonResults is zero,
            // exit with nil
            if (!resultCount){
              completionBlock(nil);
              return;
            }

            NSDictionary *appDetails = [[jsonResults ↵
                                              objectForKey: @"results"] ↵
                            firstObject];

            NSString *latestVersion = [appDetails ↵
                                              objectForKey: @"version"];

            completionBlock(latestVersion);

          }] resume];
}
```

You must use it like this

```
[self getAppVersionAndRunOnCompletion:^(NSString *version) {
    NSLog(@"latest version on the app store = %@", version);
}];
```

Breakpoints and NSLog Not Working

When this problem occurs, Xcode will not stop on any defined breakpoint and, as a bonus, NSLog will not print anything to Xcode's console.

This problem is generally a result of one of two issues: a corrupted project file or a bad product scheme.

For some reason, application extensions and Apple Watch targets are more likely to be affected by bad product schemes.

> **Note**   Xcode loses control of things and product schemes are corrupted if you create and delete targets several times during the project.

Project corruption

First, try to clean the project by following the instructions found in the section "Xcode Crashing when Opening a Project File?" and see if the problem is solved.

Bad product scheme

If the problem is not solved, click **Product ➤ Scheme ➤ Manage Schemes**, select all schemes, and delete them by clicking the **minus sign** at the bottom left. Then click the **Autocreate Schemes Now** button to re-create the schemes you just deleted.

You can now build and run your project and the breakpoints will probably work.

Slow Transitions Between ViewControllers

If your application is using storyboards and the transitions between ViewControllers are taking too long, it is probably because iOS is having a hard time loading and instantiating the next ViewController. Perhaps the next ViewController has many elements that have to be loaded and it is taking too long.

The logical solution to that problem would be to preload the next ViewController, but how do you do that?

We have seen pages on the Web telling you to use UIPageViewControllers instead of storyboards to have smooth transitions between your ViewControllers, but this is far from being a good solution and will just create more problems.

Storyboards do not offer a way to preload ViewControllers, but we can simulate that by using the code shown here in the viewWillAppear method of the current ViewController.

Swift

```swift
override func viewWillAppear(animated: Bool) {
  super.viewWillAppear(animated)

  // This will preload the next ViewController
  dispatch_async(dispatch_get_main_queue()) {
   storyboard?.instantiateViewControllerWithIdentifier ↩
          ("nextViewController")
  }
}
```

Objective-C

```objc
- (void)viewWillAppear:(BOOL)animated {
  [super viewWillAppear:animated];

  // This will preload the next ViewController
  dispatch_async(dispatch_get_main_queue(),
  ^{
    [self.storyboard ↩
     instantiateViewControllerWithIdentifier:↩
     @"nextViewController"];
  });
}
```

This code will instantiate the next ViewController on a separate thread, which will be kept in memory. When we push the next ViewController it will load quickly and smoothly.

Finished Running Problem

You build and run your Mac or iOS application. Xcode compiles everything correctly. Xcode shows the following messages: "Building MyGreatApp..." and "Running MyGreatApp" and immediately after that terminates the application showing "Finished Running MyGreatApp." No error messages, no crash, no nothing, and also no application running.

We have warned you about the punishments

As we have said before, when the Gods punish you, they prevent Xcode from presenting any error message that can hint about the problem. But we can annoy these supreme entities and have the last laugh by thinking outside the box.

We know that OS X's console always shows error messages from applications running on the system, including Xcode. So, this is the first thing we have to check.

Console is a log viewer present on all versions of UNIX, including Mac OS X. It allows users to search through all of the system's logged messages and can alert the user when certain types of messages are logged.

To launch console, click OS X's Spotlight, type console, and press the Return key.

Keep the console window open, build and run your application again, and see if any message pops up about your application. In our case, we saw an entry like the following:

```
taskgated[98]: killed com.myGreatApp because its use of the com.apple.
developer.ubiquity-container-identifiers entitlement is not allowed (error
code -67050)
```

In other words, our application was killed by taskgated for trying to use a functionality not authorized by its entitlements. In other words, OS X killed our application for trying to do something that was not authorized by its entitlements. The question is, What exactly was it?

For some strange reason that just confirms that Xcode really hates us, a key called Ubiquity Container Identifiers was randomly added to our application's entitlements, without our knowledge and against our wishes, we swear.

To check if your application has something wrong with its entitlements, localize and open the application's entitlements window by selecting the file on Xcode's `Project Navigator`. Figure 40 shows the file and an example of entitlements.

In Figure 40, you can see that a key called `Ubiquity Container Identifiers` exists in the application's entitlements file, but this key is empty and has no value.

Figure 40. Ubiquity Container Identifiers

When you remove the key, the application works again.

If your problem is not related to the application's entitlement, the messages on console can give you clues about it.

Handoff Between iOS and Mac Clogged

This is one of the hardest problems we have ever encountered.

You are developing an iOS and an OS X version of the same application and you want to use Handoff to transfer activities between platforms.

Everything is working fine, but suddenly the plumbing between iOS and Mac applications clogs and Handoff stops working. Your iOS application posts new Handoff activities, but OS X does not respond to them.

We have prepared a systematic list of everything you must correct to unblock the pipes.

On your iOS device

1. Press the device's **Home Button** to go to the **Home Screen**.

2. Tap **Settings ➤ General ➤ Handoff & Suggested Apps** and see if **Handoff**, **My Apps,** and **App Store** are **on** (see items from ❶ to ❻ in Figures 41, 42, 43, and 44).

Figure 41. Shameless advertising showing applications created by the author and the Home Screen

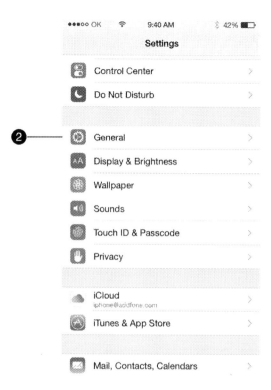

Figure 42. Settings

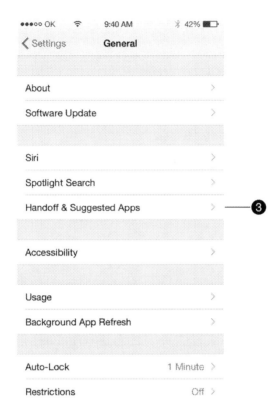

Figure 43. Handoff & suggested apps

Figure 44. Handoff

3. Make sure **Wi-Fi** and **Bluetooth** are configured and working on your device.

4. Verify if you have a working Internet connection.

On your Mac

1. Check if your Mac supports Handoff. Tap ➤ **About This Mac** ➤ **System Report** ➤ **Bluetooth** and check if **Handoff Supported** entry shows as **Yes** (Figure 45).

Figure 45. Handoff supported

2. Verify if **Bluetooth** is **on**.

3. Verify if you have a working Internet connection.

On Mac OS X

You can increase the verbosity level of sharingd (the daemon responsible for Handoff, among other things) by restarting OS X after setting a sneaky preference flag. For that matter, launch Terminal, type the following command, and press the **Return** key.

```
defaults write com.apple.Sharing EnableDebugLogging -bool TRUE
```

OS X will show sharingd messages on Console.

On your project

1. Your Mac application must be sandboxed and signed with your **Team ID**. Turn on **App Sandbox** in the **Capabilities** tab of your OS X target.

2. Check if you have added keys like the following ones to the Info.plist file:

```
<key>NSUserActivityTypes</key>
<array>
    <string>XXXXX</string>
</array>
```

    where XXXXX is the activity described like com.myCompany.myApp.activity.

3. Check if you are updating the NSUserActivity by using addUserInfoEntriesFromDictionary. Do not update the userInfo dictionary directly.

Stubborn App's Ubiquitous Container

Your application is using iCloud Drive, but the folders and files you create are not exposed publicly on iCloud.

Debugging iCloud is a complex task, especially because the only tool available for that matter on Xcode is the **iCloud Debug Gauge** (Figure 46), and that gauge has been broken since Xcode 6. Chances are that the gauge will show your app's iCloud status as Disabled (**❶**) all the time.

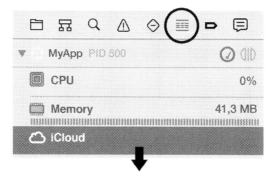

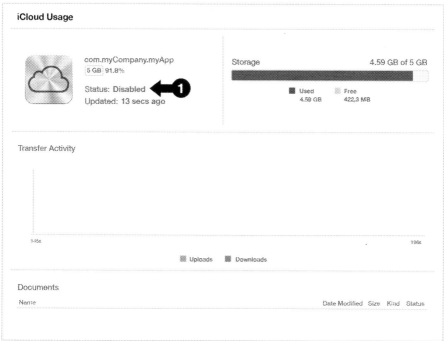

Figure 46. iCloud debug gauge

Verify this

Here are a few things you should verify to expose your application's folder on iCloud:

1. iCloud capability must be turned on for iCloud Documents using the default container or some custom container you have defined.

2. The entitlements file must be something like the following:

```
<key>com.apple.developer.icloud-container- ↵
                identifiers</key>
<array>
    <string>iCloud.$(CFBundleIdentifier)</string>
</array>
<key>com.apple.developer.icloud-services</key>
<array>
    <string>CloudDocuments</string>
</array>
<key>com.apple.developer.ubiquity-container- ↵
            identifiers</key>
<array/>
```

3. Have you added keys like these to the Info.plist file?

```
<key>NSUbiquitousContainers</key>
<dict>
    <key>iCloud.$(CFBundleIdentifier)</key>
    <dict>
    <key>NSUbiquitousContainerIsDocumentScopePublic</key>
    <true/>
    <key>NSUbiquitousContainerSupportedFolderLevels</key>
    <string>Any</string>
    <key>NSUbiquitousContainerName</key>
    <string>MyApp</string>
</dict>
```

Here comes the secret "spell" ...

Every time you change something on your application's iCloud configuration, like the container name or container identifier, increase your application Info.plist's version and build –CFBundleShortVersionString and

CFBundleVersion, respectively, and make sure your application runs the following line at launch:

```
[[NSFileManager defaultManager] ↩ URLForUbiquityContainerIdentifier:nil];
```

> **Note**   Mac OS X comes with a tool called `brctl`, which is a manager for the `CloudDocs` daemon and responsible for transferring files from your device to iCloud.
>
> To use this tool, launch `Terminal`, type the following command, and press the Return key:
>
> `brctl log --wait --shorten`

Where you can see the files...

Once the files and folders are exposed on the iCloud Drive, you can see them in any of the following places:

1. On your device's **Settings ➤ iCloud ➤ Manage Storage ➤ Documents & Data**;

2. On Mac OS X's iCloud Drive folder;

3. Inside your application by using `UIDocumentPicker` called by the following code:

Swift

```
@IBAction func openImportDocumentPicker(sender : AnyObject) {

    let documentPicker = UIDocumentPickerViewController ↩
        (documentTypes: ["public.image"], ↩
                    inMode: UIDocumentPickerMode.Import)

    documentPicker.modalPresentationStyle = ↩
                                    UIModalPresentationStyle.FormSheet

    self.presentViewController(documentPicker, animated: true)
    { () -> Void in  }
}
```

Objective-C

```objectivec
- (IBAction)openImportDocumentPicker:(id)sender {

    UIDocumentPickerViewController *documentPicker = ↵
                        [[UIDocumentPickerViewController alloc] ↵
                            initWithDocumentTypes:@[@"public.image"] ↵
                inMode:UIDocumentPickerModeImport];

    documentPicker.modalPresentationStyle = ↵
                        UIModalPresentationFormSheet;

    [self presentViewController:documentPicker
                    animated:YES completion:nil];
}
```

Power Tips

Making life easier for a developer involves not only solving problems inside Xcode, as this book has tried to do, but also doing things and using tools outside Xcode that can help development.

The following sections review some of these tools.

CocoaPods

According to CocoaPods' web site, CocoaPods is the dependency manager for Swift and Objective-C Cocoa projects. It has almost 10,000 libraries and can help you scale your projects elegantly.

Briefly, CocoaPods is a huge archive containing thousands of libraries and open source code that you can use on your projects—code that will not only accelerate development but also make development easier.

It is very easy to use CocoaPods on your projects, and there are a lot of tutorials on the Web that explain it.

`www.cocoapods.org`

GitHub

Another good source for open source code for your projects is GitHub. Many projects hosted with GitHub can be easily imported into your projects using CocoaPods. So, don't forget to check them out:

`www.github.com`

StackOverflow

If everything else fails, try StackOverflow.

Following is StackOverflow's own official definition: "Stack Overflow is a question and answer site for professional and enthusiast programmers. It's built and run by you as part of the Stack Exchange network of Q&A sites. With your help, we're working together to build a library of detailed answers to every question about programming."

StackOverflow is to our knowledge the best web site for posting questions and getting fast and high-quality answers.

`www.stackoverflow.com`

fastlane Tools

According to fastlane's web site, "fastlane lets you define and run your deployment pipelines for different environments. It helps you unify your app's release process and automate the whole process. fastlane connects all fastlane tools and third-party tools, like CocoaPods and xctool."

By saying "automate the whole process," fastlane means using Terminal to do a lot of things related to the development and delivery of your apps and removing the Calvary and suffering related with dealing with iTunesConnect and with the Developer Portal, including the provisioning profiles nightmare.

```
http://fastlane.tools
```

HandBrake

HandBrake is an open source tool for converting videos from nearly any format to a selection of modern, widely supported codecs. We have seen Handbrake converting videos that are 1.2GB in size up to 16 Mb with no noticeable loss in picture quality.

```
http://handbrake.fr
```

Alcatraz

According to Alcatraz's web site, "Alcatraz is an open source package manager for Xcode. It lets you discover and install plug-ins, templates, and color schemes without the need for manually cloning or copying files."

In other words, Alcatraz lets you install a lot of useful plug-ins that help you improve Xcode.

```
www.alcatraz.io
```

Appendix

The following table provides all the NSLocale codes used by Apple devices for localizations.

Apple uses the codes created by the International Organization for Standardization (ISO), which is an independent, nongovernmental membership organization and the world's largest developer of voluntary international standards. Visit www.iso.org for more information.

The table in this appendix is a compilation of the ISO codes and shows generic entries like "en" for "English" and specific ones like "en_AU" for "Australian English" or "en_JM" for "Jamaican English." The English language, itself, has almost 30 variations. If you use a specific one, that localization will only be visible if the device is adjusted for using that variation. By using the generic "en," you guarantee that all devices adjusted with a variation of English will see the localization. That is also true when you create localizations on the App Store from iTunesConnect.

NSLocale	Country
af	Afrikaans
af_NA	Afrikaans (Namibia)
af_ZA	Afrikaans (South Africa)
ak	Akan
ak_GH	Akan (Ghana)
sq	Albanian
sq_AL	Albanian (Albania)
am	Amharic
am_ET	Amharic (Ethiopia)
ar	Arabic
ar_DZ	Arabic (Algeria)
ar_BH	Arabic (Bahrain)
ar_EG	Arabic (Egypt)
ar_IQ	Arabic (Iraq)
ar_JO	Arabic (Jordan)
ar_KW	Arabic (Kuwait)
ar_LB	Arabic (Lebanon)

(continued)

NSLocale	Country
ar_LY	Arabic (Libya)
ar_MA	Arabic (Morocco)
ar_OM	Arabic (Oman)
ar_QA	Arabic (Qatar)
ar_SA	Arabic (Saudi Arabia)
ar_SD	Arabic (Sudan)
ar_SY	Arabic (Syria)
ar_TN	Arabic (Tunisia)
ar_AE	Arabic (United Arab Emirates)
ar_YE	Arabic (Yemen)
hy	Armenian
hy_AM	Armenian (Armenia)
as	Assamese
as_IN	Assamese (India)
asa	Asu
asa_TZ	Asu (Tanzania)
az	Azerbaijani
az_Cyrl_AZ	Azerbaijani (Cyrillic, Azerbaijan)
az_Cyrl	Azerbaijani (Cyrillic)
az_Latn_AZ	Azerbaijani (Latin, Azerbaijan)
az_Latn	Azerbaijani (Latin)
bm	Bambara
bm_ML	Bambara (Mali)
eu	Basque
eu_ES	Basque (Spain)
be	Belarusian
be_BY	Belarusian (Belarus)
bem	Bemba
bem_ZM	Bemba (Zambia)
bez	Bena
bez_TZ	Bena (Tanzania)

(continued)

NSLocale	Country
bn	Bengali
bn_BD	Bengali (Bangladesh)
bn_IN	Bengali (India)
bs	Bosnian
bs_BA	Bosnian (Bosnia and Herzegovina)
bg	Bulgarian
bg_BG	Bulgarian (Bulgaria)
my	Burmese
my_MM	Burmese (Myanmar [Burma])
ca	Catalan
ca_ES	Catalan (Spain)
tzm	Central Morocco Tamazight
tzm_Latn_MA	Central Morocco Tamazight (Latin, Morocco)
tzm_Latn	Central Morocco Tamazight (Latin)
chr	Cherokee
chr_US	Cherokee (United States)
cgg	Chiga
cgg_UG	Chiga (Uganda)
zh	Chinese
zh_Hans_CN	Chinese (Simplified Han, China)
zh_Hans_HK	Chinese (Simplified Han, Hong Kong SAR China)
zh_Hans_MO	Chinese (Simplified Han, Macau SAR China)
zh_Hans_SG	Chinese (Simplified Han, Singapore)
zh_Hans	Chinese (Simplified Han)
zh_Hant_HK	Chinese (Traditional Han, Hong Kong SAR China)
zh_Hant_MO	Chinese (Traditional Han, Macau SAR China)
zh_Hant_TW	Chinese (Traditional Han, Taiwan)
zh_Hant	Chinese (Traditional Han)
kw	Cornish
kw_GB	Cornish (United Kingdom)
hr	Croatian

(continued)

NSLocale	Country
hr_HR	Croatian (Croatia)
cs	Czech
cs_CZ	Czech (Czech Republic)
da	Danish
da_DK	Danish (Denmark)
nl	Dutch
nl_BE	Dutch (Belgium)
nl_NL	Dutch (Netherlands)
ebu	Embu
ebu_KE	Embu (Kenya)
en	English
en_AS	English (American Samoa)
en_AU	English (Australia)
en_BE	English (Belgium)
en_BZ	English (Belize)
en_BW	English (Botswana)
en_CA	English (Canada)
en_GU	English (Guam)
en_HK	English (Hong Kong SAR China)
en_IN	English (India)
en_IE	English (Ireland)
en_JM	English (Jamaica)
en_MT	English (Malta)
en_MH	English (Marshall Islands)
en_MU	English (Mauritius)
en_NA	English (Namibia)
en_NZ	English (New Zealand)
en_MP	English (Northern Mariana Islands)
en_PK	English (Pakistan)
en_PH	English (Philippines)
en_SG	English (Singapore)

(continued)

NSLocale	Country
en_ZA	English (South Africa)
en_TT	English (Trinidad and Tobago)
en_UM	English (U.S. Minor Outlying Islands)
en_VI	English (U.S. Virgin Islands)
en_GB	English (United Kingdom)
en_US_POSIX	English (United States, Computer)
en_US	English (United States)
en_ZW	English (Zimbabwe)
eo	Esperanto
et	Estonian
et_EE	Estonian (Estonia)
ee	Ewe
ee_GH	Ewe (Ghana)
ee_TG	Ewe (Togo)
fo	Faroese
fo_FO	Faroese (Faroe Islands)
fil	Filipino
fil_PH	Filipino (Philippines)
fi	Finnish
fi_FI	Finnish (Finland)
fr	French
fr_BE	French (Belgium)
fr_BJ	French (Benin)
fr_BF	French (Burkina Faso)
fr_BI	French (Burundi)
fr_CM	French (Cameroon)
fr_CA	French (Canada)
fr_CF	French (Central African Republic)
fr_TD	French (Chad)
fr_KM	French (Comoros)
fr_CG	French (Congo - Brazzaville)

(continued)

NSLocale	Country
fr_CD	French (Congo - Kinshasa)
fr_CI	French (Côte d'Ivoire)
fr_DJ	French (Djibouti)
fr_GQ	French (Equatorial Guinea)
fr_FR	French (France)
fr_GA	French (Gabon)
fr_GP	French (Guadeloupe)
fr_GN	French (Guinea)
fr_LU	French (Luxembourg)
fr_MG	French (Madagascar)
fr_ML	French (Mali)
fr_MQ	French (Martinique)
fr_MC	French (Monaco)
fr_NE	French (Niger)
fr_RE	French (Réunion)
fr_RW	French (Rwanda)
fr_BL	French (Saint Barthélemy)
fr_MF	French (Saint Martin)
fr_SN	French (Senegal)
fr_CH	French (Switzerland)
fr_TG	French (Togo)
ff	Fulah
ff_SN	Fulah (Senegal)
gl	Galician
gl_ES	Galician (Spain)
lg	Ganda
lg_UG	Ganda (Uganda)
ka	Georgian
ka_GE	Georgian (Georgia)
de	German
de_AT	German (Austria)

(continued)

NSLocale	Country
de_BE	German (Belgium)
de_DE	German (Germany)
de_LI	German (Liechtenstein)
de_LU	German (Luxembourg)
de_CH	German (Switzerland)
el	Greek
el_CY	Greek (Cyprus)
el_GR	Greek (Greece)
gu	Gujarati
gu_IN	Gujarati (India)
guz	Gusii
guz_KE	Gusii (Kenya)
ha	Hausa
ha_Latn_GH	Hausa (Latin, Ghana)
ha_Latn_NE	Hausa (Latin, Niger)
ha_Latn_NG	Hausa (Latin, Nigeria)
ha_Latn	Hausa (Latin)
haw	Hawaiian
haw_US	Hawaiian (United States)
he	Hebrew
he_IL	Hebrew (Israel)
hi	Hindi
hi_IN	Hindi (India)
hu	Hungarian
hu_HU	Hungarian (Hungary)
is	Icelandic
is_IS	Icelandic (Iceland)
ig	Igbo
ig_NG	Igbo (Nigeria)
id	Indonesian
id_ID	Indonesian (Indonesia)

(continued)

NSLocale	Country
ga	Irish
ga_IE	Irish (Ireland)
it	Italian
it_IT	Italian (Italy)
it_CH	Italian (Switzerland)
ja	Japanese
ja_JP	Japanese (Japan)
kea	Kabuverdianu
kea_CV	Kabuverdianu (Cape Verde)
kab	Kabyle
kab_DZ	Kabyle (Algeria)
kl	Kalaallisut
kl_GL	Kalaallisut (Greenland)
kln	Kalenjin
kln_KE	Kalenjin (Kenya)
kam	Kamba
kam_KE	Kamba (Kenya)
kn	Kannada
kn_IN	Kannada (India)
kk	Kazakh
kk_Cyrl_KZ	Kazakh (Cyrillic, Kazakhstan)
kk_Cyrl	Kazakh (Cyrillic)
km	Khmer
km_KH	Khmer (Cambodia)
ki	Kikuyu
ki_KE	Kikuyu (Kenya)
rw	Kinyarwanda
rw_RW	Kinyarwanda (Rwanda)
kok	Konkani
kok_IN	Konkani (India)
ko	Korean

(continued)

NSLocale	Country
ko_KR	Korean (South Korea)
khq	Koyra Chiini
khq_ML	Koyra Chiini (Mali)
ses	Koyraboro Senni
ses_ML	Koyraboro Senni (Mali)
lag	Langi
lag_TZ	Langi (Tanzania)
lv	Latvian
lv_LV	Latvian (Latvia)
lt	Lithuanian
lt_LT	Lithuanian (Lithuania)
luo	Luo
luo_KE	Luo (Kenya)
luy	Luyia
luy_KE	Luyia (Kenya)
mk	Macedonian
mk_MK	Macedonian (Macedonia)
jmc	Machame
jmc_TZ	Machame (Tanzania)
kde	Makonde
kde_TZ	Makonde (Tanzania)
mg	Malagasy
mg_MG	Malagasy (Madagascar)
ms	Malay
ms_BN	Malay (Brunei)
ms_MY	Malay (Malaysia)
ml	Malayalam
ml_IN	Malayalam (India)
mt	Maltese
mt_MT	Maltese (Malta)
gv	Manx

(continued)

NSLocale	Country
gv_GB	Manx (United Kingdom)
mr	Marathi
mr_IN	Marathi (India)
mas	Masai
mas_KE	Masai (Kenya)
mas_TZ	Masai (Tanzania)
mer	Meru
mer_KE	Meru (Kenya)
mfe	Morisyen
mfe_MU	Morisyen (Mauritius)
naq	Nama
naq_NA	Nama (Namibia)
ne	Nepali
ne_IN	Nepali (India)
ne_NP	Nepali (Nepal)
nd	North Ndebele
nd_ZW	North Ndebele (Zimbabwe)
nb	Norwegian Bokmål
nb_NO	Norwegian Bokmål (Norway)
nn	Norwegian Nynorsk
nn_NO	Norwegian Nynorsk (Norway)
nyn	Nyankole
nyn_UG	Nyankole (Uganda)
or	Oriya
or_IN	Oriya (India)
om	Oromo
om_ET	Oromo (Ethiopia)
om_KE	Oromo (Kenya)
ps	Pashto
ps_AF	Pashto (Afghanistan)
fa	Persian

(continued)

NSLocale	Country
fa_AF	Persian (Afghanistan)
fa_IR	Persian (Iran)
pl	Polish
pl_PL	Polish (Poland)
pt	Portuguese
pt_BR	Portuguese (Brazil)
pt_GW	Portuguese (Guinea-Bissau)
pt_MZ	Portuguese (Mozambique)
pt_PT	Portuguese (Portugal)
pa	Punjabi
pa_Arab_PK	Punjabi (Arabic, Pakistan)
pa_Arab	Punjabi (Arabic)
pa_Guru_IN	Punjabi (Gurmukhi, India)
pa_Guru	Punjabi (Gurmukhi)
ro	Romanian
ro_MD	Romanian (Moldova)
ro_RO	Romanian (Romania)
rm	Romansh
rm_CH	Romansh (Switzerland)
rof	Rombo
rof_TZ	Rombo (Tanzania)
ru	Russian
ru_MD	Russian (Moldova)
ru_RU	Russian (Russia)
ru_UA	Russian (Ukraine)
rwk	Rwa
rwk_TZ	Rwa (Tanzania)
saq	Samburu
saq_KE	Samburu (Kenya)
sg	Sango
sg_CF	Sango (Central African Republic)

(continued)

NSLocale	Country
seh	Sena
seh_MZ	Sena (Mozambique)
sr	Serbian
sr_Cyrl_BA	Serbian (Cyrillic, Bosnia and Herzegovina)
sr_Cyrl_ME	Serbian (Cyrillic, Montenegro)
sr_Cyrl_RS	Serbian (Cyrillic, Serbia)
sr_Cyrl	Serbian (Cyrillic)
sr_Latn_BA	Serbian (Latin, Bosnia and Herzegovina)
sr_Latn_ME	Serbian (Latin, Montenegro)
sr_Latn_RS	Serbian (Latin, Serbia)
sr_Latn	Serbian (Latin)
sn	Shona
sn_ZW	Shona (Zimbabwe)
ii	Sichuan Yi
ii_CN	Sichuan Yi (China)
si	Sinhala
si_LK	Sinhala (Sri Lanka)
sk	Slovak
sk_SK	Slovak (Slovakia)
sl	Slovenian
sl_SI	Slovenian (Slovenia)
xog	Soga
xog_UG	Soga (Uganda)
so	Somali
so_DJ	Somali (Djibouti)
so_ET	Somali (Ethiopia)
so_KE	Somali (Kenya)
so_SO	Somali (Somalia)
es	Spanish
es_AR	Spanish (Argentina)
es_BO	Spanish (Bolivia)

(continued)

NSLocale	Country
es_CL	Spanish (Chile)
es_CO	Spanish (Colombia)
es_CR	Spanish (Costa Rica)
es_DO	Spanish (Dominican Republic)
es_EC	Spanish (Ecuador)
es_SV	Spanish (El Salvador)
es_GQ	Spanish (Equatorial Guinea)
es_GT	Spanish (Guatemala)
es_HN	Spanish (Honduras)
es_419	Spanish (Latin America)
es_MX	Spanish (Mexico)
es_NI	Spanish (Nicaragua)
es_PA	Spanish (Panama)
es_PY	Spanish (Paraguay)
es_PE	Spanish (Peru)
es_PR	Spanish (Puerto Rico)
es_ES	Spanish (Spain)
es_US	Spanish (United States)
es_UY	Spanish (Uruguay)
es_VE	Spanish (Venezuela)
sw	Swahili
sw_KE	Swahili (Kenya)
sw_TZ	Swahili (Tanzania)
sv	Swedish
sv_FI	Swedish (Finland)
sv_SE	Swedish (Sweden)
gsw	Swiss German
gsw_CH	Swiss German (Switzerland)
shi	Tachelhit
shi_Latn_MA	Tachelhit (Latin, Morocco)
shi_Latn	Tachelhit (Latin)

(continued)

NSLocale	Country
shi_Tfng_MA	Tachelhit (Tifinagh, Morocco)
shi_Tfng	Tachelhit (Tifinagh)
dav	Taita
dav_KE	Taita (Kenya)
ta	Tamil
ta_IN	Tamil (India)
ta_LK	Tamil (Sri Lanka)
te	Telugu
te_IN	Telugu (India)
teo	Teso
teo_KE	Teso (Kenya)
teo_UG	Teso (Uganda)
th	Thai
th_TH	Thai (Thailand)
bo	Tibetan
bo_CN	Tibetan (China)
bo_IN	Tibetan (India)
ti	Tigrinya
ti_ER	Tigrinya (Eritrea)
ti_ET	Tigrinya (Ethiopia)
to	Tonga
to_TO	Tonga (Tonga)
tr	Turkish
tr_TR	Turkish (Turkey)
uk	Ukrainian
uk_UA	Ukrainian (Ukraine)
ur	Urdu
ur_IN	Urdu (India)
ur_PK	Urdu (Pakistan)
uz	Uzbek
uz_Arab_AF	Uzbek (Arabic, Afghanistan)

(continued)

NSLocale	Country
uz_Arab	Uzbek (Arabic)
uz_Cyrl_UZ	Uzbek (Cyrillic, Uzbekistan)
uz_Cyrl	Uzbek (Cyrillic)
uz_Latn_UZ	Uzbek (Latin, Uzbekistan)
uz_Latn	Uzbek (Latin)
vi	Vietnamese
vi_VN	Vietnamese (Vietnam)
vun	Vunjo
vun_TZ	Vunjo (Tanzania)
cy	Welsh
cy_GB	Welsh (United Kingdom)
yo	Yoruba
yo_NG	Yoruba (Nigeria)
zu	Zulu
zu_ZA	Zulu (South Africa)

Index

▓P, Q

Provisioning profile, 30

▓R

Regular expressions, 42
    Find field, 41, 43
    Replace field, 41, 44
    search command, 45
RenderMe
    absolute paths, 31
    expectations, 31

▓S

SBPartialInfo
    duplicate reference, 9
    error message, 6
    Info.plist file
        incorrect path, 7
        target, 8
    NSLayoutConstraint, 6
signal SIGABRT message, 38
Signing identity, 4
Size Classes selection, 81
SpriteKit
    didBeginContact method, 58
    physicsBody boundary
        convex shape, 59
        non-convex shape, 60
StackOverflow, 105

▓T

tintColor property, 24

▓U

Ubiquity Container
        Identifiers, 94
UIButton
    disabled, 55
    enabled, 55
UIPickerView
    Objective-C, 72
    Swift, 72
UI_USER_INTERFACE_IDIOM()
    method, 51
UIView base class
    objective-C, 64
    Swift, 63
UIViews and NSViews
    objective-C, 69
    Swift, 66

▓V, W, X, Y, Z

ViewControllers, 50, 92
    objective-C, 92
    Swift, 92
    UIPageView
        Controllers, 92
    viewWillAppear
        method, 92

Get the eBook for only $5!

Why limit yourself?

Now you can take the weightless companion with you wherever you go and access your content on your PC, phone, tablet, or reader.

Since you've purchased this print book, we're happy to offer you the eBook in all 3 formats for just $5.

Convenient and fully searchable, the PDF version enables you to easily find and copy code—or perform examples by quickly toggling between instructions and applications. The MOBI format is ideal for your Kindle, while the ePUB can be utilized on a variety of mobile devices.

To learn more, go to www.apress.com/companion or contact support@apress.com.

Printed in the United States
By Bookmasters